# MYRNA LOY

# MYRNA LOY

*A Pyramid Illustrated History of the Movies*

**by**
**KARYN KAY**

***General Editor:* TED SENNETT**

*To my mother and father,*
*Miriam and Henry,*
*with love*

**MYRNA LOY**
**A Pyramid History of the Movies**

**A PYRAMID BOOK**



Pyramid edition published April 1977

Library of Congress Catalog Card Number: 77-73158

Printed in the United States of America

---

Pyramid Books are published by Pyramid Publications (Harcourt Brace Jovanovich, Inc.). Its trademarks, consisting of the word "Pyramid" and the portrayal of a pyramid, are registered in the United States Patent Office.

PYRAMID PUBLICATIONS
(Harcourt Brace Jovanovich, Inc.)
757 Third Avenue, New York, N.Y. 10017

**(graphic design by Anthony Basile)**

# ACKNOWLEDGMENTS

My thanks to research assistant Dannis Peary and to Christine Nielson of the *Chicago Daily News*; to Kathy Koch and Roger Shatzkin for their extra contributions; Bill Horrigan, Stuart Kaminsky, and my friends at Northwestern University; Elizabeth Dalton and the staff of the University of Wisconsin Center for Theater Research; Charles Silver, Steve Harvey and the staff at the Museum of Modern Art Film Archive; Myra, Linda and Gail and Steve, Walter, and Rachel; Andy, Barbara and the "little" Sheehys; Barry Brown, Jeanine Basinger, Peter Farrell. Thanks especially to the folks at Films Inc. in Wilmette—to Doug Lemza, a hug extravaganza—and to my editor, Ted Sennett, for kindness beyond reason.

Last, thanks to Jerry.

Photographs: Jerry Vermilye, The Memory Shop,
Eddie Brandt's Saturday Matinee, and
the companies that produced and distributed
the films of Myrna Loy

# CONTENTS

# INTRODUCTION

M*yrna Loy*. John Dillinger lost his life for her. The dashing bandit, reportedly stuck on the star, returned three times to watch Myrna perform in *Manhattan Melodrama* (1934). After the third viewing, he was gunned down by G-Men's bullets outside Chicago's Clark Theater.

Myrna Loy was also Franklin Roosevelt's favorite actress. The President was "terribly distressed," in Eleanor's words, to have missed sharing a birthday celebration with Myrna. He was off in Teheran on business when she arrived at the White House, sporting a new John Frederick hat in tribute to F.D.R.

Myrna Loy also had an ardent fan in author F. Scott Fitzgerald. He considered her for the role of Nicole Diver in a personally cast film version of his novel, *Tender is the Night*. Sadly, Fitzgerald's pet project was never realized in his lifetime.

Into 1977, Myrna Loy has made well over one hundred films and turned down dozens more—including *It Happened One Night* (1934). She vamped through the first half of her career, typecast as an exotic seductress of anomolous Third World descent. Early Myrna was a heartless vagabond, whose tramp sexuality was the torment of many a young innocent. In *The Squall* (1929), she ruined a happy family, pitting father against son in thirst for her mad gypsy, Nubi. Selfish gadabout, she jilted one man after another, leaving Robert Ames to marry good Ina Claire by default in *Rebound* (1931) and abandoning Pat O'Brien to sweet Irene Dunne in *Consolation Marriage* (1931). Even in the pleasant *A Connecticut Yankee* (1931), with Will Rogers, Myrna found a villainous part to inhabit—the mean Morgan Le Fay, who lovingly hanged her myriad male victims.

In her Third World period, Myrna was a mystagogue, a siren and scourge in league with death, plundering the earth on the way to her own almost fated demise. In John Ford's *The Black Watch* (1929), she is Yasmini of India, a savage leader of a band of renegades and slaves, who perishes for love of Britain's Victor McLaglen. In *The Mask of Fu Manchu* (1932), she is the evil Oriental's devilish daughter, in Loy's words, "a sadistic nymphomaniac," who succumbs in the middle of a riot. As a Javanese occultist in *Thirteen Women* (1932), she causes the death of nine sorority sisters as revenge against their school girl racism before plunging off a moving train herself. In *Renegades* (1930), Myrna plays a spy who leads an insurgent band of legionnaires on a predictable trip

to the grave. Everyone dies in this movie, including Myrna. Mortally wounded, she goes out in typically tempestuous fashion, kissing her ex-lover on the mouth while shooting him in the belly. Mickey Spillane couldn't have done it better.

Myrna retired from vamping deep into her career with the production of *The Prizefighter and the Lady* (1933). This was Myrna's first film under the direction of W. S. Van Dyke, and, with their second together, *Penthouse* (1933), Van Dyke smoothly accomplished Myrna's metamorphosis from slinky homewrecker to sensuous homemaker, making enlightened use of Loy's old vamp image upon which to build the chorus girl/prostitute Gertie. Gertie is the quintessential golden-hearted whore, risking her life to help her man, wealthy Warner Baxter, nab the killer gangster. At *Penthouse*'s conclusion, Gertie is rewarded with Warner Baxter's love and the proverbial "second chance" in matrimony to the rich attorney.

Upward mobility inevitably translated as marriage in her post-1933 films, but a marriage of surprising spirit and fun. It was a short but irreversible skip from ghetto strumpet to live-wire Park Avenue matron—slumming in Harlem, enjoying whiskey and jazz uptown, then home to tea at the Plaza. Nubi's wild paisley tunic of *The Squall* was exchanged comfortably and unregrettably for a Saks brocade lounging gown.

Myrna Loy recounts that after the filming of *Penthouse*, director Woody Van Dyke made a very daring public prophecy about her future at MGM, the king of film studios. She reports he told her: "Within a year I would have a starring role. I didn't believe it myself."

He more than kept his promise, not only finding a starring part for Loy but making Myrna Loy herself a Star. In 1934, Van Dyke perfectly cast Myrna Loy as "perfect wife" to William Powell's Nick Charles. The movie was *The Thin Man*, from the detective novel by Dashiell Hammett, and from it sprang the immortal series. Altogether Myrna was Powell's partner six times as Nick's irrepressible Nora. They were such a smashing team that they were coupled eight more times in *Manhattan Melodrama* (1934), *Evelyn Prentice* (1934), *The Great Ziegfeld* (1936), *Libeled Lady* (1936), *Double Wedding* (1937), *I Love You Again* (1940), *Love Crazy* (1941), and, finally, *The Senator Was Indiscreet* (1947). In this final film, William Powell plays the lead role as the senator, and Loy shows up as an unbilled surprise at the film's close to portray, naturally, the senator's wife. Like hot and cold, yin and yang, Nick and Nora, the name Loy suggests the name Powell.

Powell was the perfect mate for Loy, but the moviegoing public associated her just as frequently with another (and bigger) MGM star. In 1936, when she was dubbed "Queen of the Movies" in Ed Sullivan's national newspaper poll, her "King" was Clark Gable. Myrna Loy and Gable teamed up seven times in *Night Flight* (1933), *Men in White* (1934), *Manhattan Melodrama* (1934), *Wife Vs. Secretary* (1936), *Parnell* (1937), *Test Pilot* (1938) and *Too Hot to Handle* (1938).

Myrna Loy was never Gable's perfect wife. They fought; they resisted each other. They did not share in gentle lovers' matches, the respectful repartée, that went on between Powell and Loy. Gable and Loy tried to transform each other. In *Men in White*, he wants to shake up and shape up Loy's spoiled heiress. In *Manhattan Melodrama*, she threatens Gable's gangster Gallagher: give up the rackets or she'll give up the gangster. She frets through *Wife Vs. Secretary* to his everlasting annoyance, and in *Test Pilot*, he wants to fly while she wants to ground him.

In an interview with David Chierichetti, Loy noted, "In all my pictures with Clark Gable . . . I had to play tough, independent women. Clark was always trying to put me on the spot . . . there was a constant oneupmanship." Their fraying was fine and meant more varied roles for Loy beyond the dandy comedies she shared with Powell. However, with Gable she never achieved the cool harmony, the joyful symmetry she enjoyed with Powell. She and Gable might have been the King and Queen by popular command, but she and Powell were a screen god and goddess by magic and wizardry.

The pages ahead chronicle, of course, not only Loy and Powell and Loy and Gable but much more of the film career of Myrna Loy. She has now been in the movies for over fifty years. But what of her private life? There is not much to tell, at least publicly. Myrna Loy has insisted always on keeping her own story out of the papers. After her first trip to the altar, Loy was annoyed at the small-mindedness of the press: "All anyone seemed to care about was my marriage. I can't see what that has to do with my work." And this attitude has prevailed.

What *has* been public is Loy's second interest, politics. A lifelong fighting liberal, she has ventured into areas where most Hollywood actors have kept their noses clean. She was a determined anti-Fascist in the thirties, a voice against Joseph McCarthy and HUAC in the forties and fifties. (Supposedly she would telegram the HUAC committee, "I dare you to ask me

to testify.") For twenty-five years she has been a public enemy of Richard M. Nixon. And even now, into her seventies, Myrna Loy remains a progressive, supporting the McGovern anti-war movement and fighting in California for open housing legislation.

What to conclude? That Myrna Loy's life outside of film has been like her life in the cinema—guided by grace, intelligence and a very open heart.

# MONTANA MYRNA

On August 2, 1905, a baby girl was born to Della and David Williams of Raidersburg, Montana. The parents called their daughter Myrna—a name taken from a sign post sighted by Papa Williams while riding a train through his home state.

David and Della were of Welsh and Scottish descent. They owned a humble cattle ranch, and their lifestyle was modest, even while Mr. Williams served in the Montana State Legislature. (He was elected to the governing body when only twenty-one years old.) In 1912, when Myrna was seven, Mr. Williams moved the family to Helena, also in Montana.

Myrna was born a Leo—the fire of her sign was displayed in her carrot-colored hair and sprawling freckles. She was not a very quiet little girl. Young Myrna Williams was a tomboy who enjoyed running bases with the boys and didn't much mind mud-splattered knees and bruised elbows. As the ex-Miss Williams recalls, "If ever there was an ugly little girl, it was I. I was . . . skinny and never once in the first few years of my life did anyone hug me or pat my head and say, 'What a lovely, luscious little girl.' At least I escaped that."

It was really not such a giant step from that plucky little orange-headed moppet, Myrna Williams, to the charming and beauteous Myrna Loy. She had, after all, decided upon a career as a great actress by age eleven. A 1916 family trip to California, which included a tour of the Universal studio, led to this momentous professional resolution. The young Myrna made her theatrical debut that fall, performing a personally created version of Sleeping Beauty for a schoolmate—Johnny Mack Brown—on whom she had a crush. With her brother David's assistance, Myrna transformed the Williams' home into the primeval forest of the fairy tale. But Johnny Mack Brown was not impressed. He just laughed. His infuriating response intensified Myrna's determination to become an actress. She persuaded her parents to allow her to take dancing lessons from a Miss Alice Thompson. That summer, Miss Thompson's star pupil was chosen to dance in a Helena fund-raising production. Later, the twelve-year-old talent repeated her "Bluebird" performance at a local army base.

In 1918, the Spanish flu epidemic hit Helena. Mr. Williams died, and, not long after, his widow Della moved with her two children to California. In 1920, Myrna Williams enrolled in Venice High School on the edges of Los Angeles. Under the tutelage of artist H. T. Winebreiner, Myrna began sculpting, and she also posed for his statue of "spiritual man" (sic), which stood in front of the high school. On Memorial Day, 1923, Loy and the statue were invited aboard the Navy ship *U.S.S. Nevada*. The publicity resulted in Myrna Williams being hired to teach at the Horsley Dance School. Friends at the academy tipped Myrna off to a hoofer's job at Grauman's Chinese Theatre. So, by the summer of 1923, not long after her high school graduation, Myrna Williams could be found salaaming in the Grauman chorus prologue for *The Ten Commandments*.

Myrna Williams simultaneously filled a friend's spot as film splicer at Warners' cutting room. Yet she was not too busy to sit in when Henry Waxman came around Grauman's to photograph the troupers. He took a fantastic picture of Myrna Williams and some sister chorines, wildly wardrobed in their most exotic costumes, then hung it on his studio wall. Knowing that Rudolph Valentino loved "discovering" people, Waxman phoned the actor to view his display.

Valentino was impressed with Myrna Williams. His wife, Natacha Rambova, was also impressed. And since Valentino was casting for his film, *Cobra*, he arranged a screen test for Myrna from Montana—the humble rancher's daughter whose first thespian attempts had been hooted

*Myrna Loy as a child*

*At left, as one of the dancing girls in the stage "prologue" preceding the showing of THE TEN COMMANDMENTS at Grauman's Chinese Theatre, 1926*

by cowboy philistine Johnny Mack Brown.

Natacha Rambova took personal charge of Myrna's screen test, choosing wardrobe and adjusting makeup, but no amount of fluttering could prepare the neophyte actress for the moment before the camera. By her own declaration, Myrna Williams's film initiation was mortifying. "I rushed out of the projection room," Loy said in a 1937 interview, "ran home and cried for hours. I was really ashamed of myself. It was so awful, I couldn't bear to face Natacha."

The actress recovered from her humiliation. When Myrna Williams learned that Natacha Rambova was casting for her forthcoming film, *What Price Beauty*, she phoned her loyal patroness, and the understanding Rambova happily gave her a small part. The scenario revolved around the "drama" of a beauty salon. The picture, released in 1928 some years after shooting, was a commercial flop, but it provided Myrna Williams with a taste of cinema. For her business in the glamor parlor, Williams wore a bizarre costume and a strange hairdo. As she described the Rambova film to David Chierichetti in an article in *Film Fan Monthly*, "The heroine dreams she is in a fantastic beauty parlor and chooses from the different looks the models are wearing. I was 'the intellectual type' with a red velvet tunic, black pants and a tight little wig, all designed by Adrian."

*Myrna Loy and Leila Hyams, broadcasting at the opening of the Sea Breeze Beach Club in June, 1927*

*Myrna Loy around 1930*

Myrna Williams had thrown over Grauman's for her anticipated Hollywood star debut, but now she was just another unemployed. She was back on the job hunt—haunting studios, prowling around agencies. "I used to sit for days in the casting office at MGM, waiting for someone to notice me," the actress remembers. Someone finally did. She won a bit part (along with ingenue Joan Crawford) in the Metro comedy, *Pretty Ladies* (1925), and she danced in the chorus line of this Follies film. *Pretty Ladies* featured ZaSu Pitts as a homely comic set on nabbing a beau. Poor Myrna Williams didn't even merit a screen credit, but she was saved from the bread lines momentarily—and then again when she appeared as an extra in *Sporting Life* (1925), directed by Maurice Tourneur.

Myrna Williams was back in the Metro casting room waiting to be rediscovered, when the casting director asked her for another screen test. Whatever hopes she had for instant stardom were instantly dashed. The man told her to forget making up; the test was only a color check for Kathleen Key's wardrobe in *Ben-Hur*. As Loy recounted the incident, "I thought, 'Well, I'm going to put on makeup anyhow, and maybe someone will notice my face.' " Crew chief Christy Cabanne caught the face above the costume and en-

*Modeling costume jewelry in a 1931 portrait for Fox*

*PRETTY LADIES (1925). Circled at left: Myrna Loy. Circled at right: Joan Crawford*

*BEN-HUR (1926). Myrna Loy is at the extreme right in the top row. In the first row, second from the right: extra Clark Gable*

couraged Williams to audition for the part of the Madonna in *Ben-Hur*. Director Fred Niblo already had cast Betty Bronson as the Holy Virgin but he assigned the Montana maiden the role of a "hedonist," a mistress to one of the senators.

Around the time of *Ben-Hur*, people started pushing Myrna to change her name—to switch to something striking, something Hollywoodish, something less mundane than Williams. She told David Chierichetti, ". . . Friends kept telling me that with Earle Williams, Kathlyn Williams . . . there were too many Williams in the business. Somebody suggested 'Myrna Lisa' . . . " To that proposal, the actress must have wrinkled her nose long and hard in what would become characteristic "Loy" fashion.

Not long after, Williams spent an afternoon reading poetry with writer Peter Rurick. Under the influence of Gertrude Stein's "sound poems," he renamed her "Loy." He felt the cadence fit her disposition and her horoscope—the temperamental Leo. "I wasn't sold on it," remembers Loy/Williams, "but I wrote 'Myrna Loy' on the back of some photographs I sent to Warner Brothers, and when I was signed there, I became Myrna Loy for good. Of course it has turned out to be a wonderful name for me, and I love it."

After *Ben-Hur*, Myrna Williams went from chariot to charity case and had to retread her steps through the casting offices and booking agencies. According to Loy in 1937, someone upstairs at Warners saw a pre-release print of *What Price Beauty* and cast her in *Satan in Sables*, starring Lowell Sherman. "There were about sixteen women in his life in that picture," said Loy. "I was the trollop who lured him to parties, broke champagne glasses and was a hellcat in general . . . After the third day of shooting, they came up to me and signed me to a contract."

# VAMP AND REVAMP

The name Myrna Loy must have wrought weird images in the heads of her new employers, the Warner Brothers. It must have conjured thoughts of liaisons in back rooms with servant girls or romance with South Sea maidens or Asian nymphs. Perhaps a Warners' occultist read her chart to the Brothers, with the fire sign lady evoking notions of unbridled sexuality and bursting volcanic passions—for it was at Warners that Loy started her stretch as screen siren.

Lewis Milestone directed Loy in her first Warners' feature, *The Caveman* (1926), a rags-to-riches story about a coal heaver transformed into an uptown gentleman after finding half of a one hundred dollar bill dropped from a Park Avenue window. Myrna Loy appears briefly as a maid, enough for *Variety* to crown her, "one of the best vamp bets yet."

The vamp casting was put aside for Loy's next effort, *Why Girls Go Back Home* (1926)—in which Clive Brook, matinee idol, snubs his hometown cronies, and Loy kicks her heels in a chorus line—but the typecasting returned in earnest with Roy Del Ruth's *Across the Pacific* (1926). Set during the Spanish-American War, Loy plays a "native girl" who trifles with Monte Blue's affections while he is away from his American home and sweetheart. That year Loy was also visible in *The Gilded Highway, The Millionaires, The Love Toy, The Exquisite Sinner* (at MGM), and as a lady-in-waiting in John Barrymore's *Don Juan*.

She began 1927 with another John Barrymore adventure film, *When a Man Loves*, and then worked again with Roy Del Ruth in his "Negro Comedy," *Ham and Eggs at the Front*. The whole cast, including Loy as the spy, acted in blackface. In 1927, Loy also had small parts in *The Climbers*, with Irene Rich, *Simple Sis*, starring Louise Fazenda, and *A Sailor's Sweetheart*.

June of 1927 found Myrna Loy dabbling with Monte Blue again, but now—for the first time in her career—she earned star billing, temporarily. Loy, the spiteful daughter, marries Monte Blue to annoy her father. The result: sour grapes and, as the title says, *Bitter Apples*, until the couple gets shipwrecked together.

1927 continued with many more bit parts for Myrna Loy. She was "the Vamp" in *Finger Prints*, Lloyd Bacon's comical gangster picture about a mail thief who refuses to divulge the hiding place of his booty to either cops or fellow gangsters. Interestingly, no one—not even Loy—remembers her presence in this film farce, except an anonymous AFI cataloguer. Loy also made a brief appearance in *The Jazz Singer* as a hoofer backing a May McAvoy number. In fact, Loy was featured enough to silently utter a single sentence in the world's first partially sound production—commenting, by way of a title, that the bashful Al Jolson should forget his crush on McAvoy.

In 1927, Loy even played a title role in *The Girl From Chicago*—really little Mary Carlton, a Southern belle come to New York to rescue her brother from the electric chair. He's been falsely accused of committing a murder really enacted by a band of hoodlums. Mary swears to expose them by gaining entrance to the gang. She feigns urban sophistication—pulling deeply on unaccustomed cigarettes—and the thugs believe she's really a mean mama from Capone City.

*The Girl From Chicago* was "real old blood and thunder," said the *Motion Picture World* critic, with "enough gunfire to route every gang nest in Chicago." After Myrna Loy saved her brother from the toaster, she earned good reviews for herself. "An attractive actress named Myrna Loy officiates as Mary Carlton," wrote the usually mordant Mordaunt Hall in *The New York Times*.

Natacha Rambova's picture, *What Price Beauty* was finally released by Pathé in 1928, and Loy

*ACROSS THE PACIFIC (1926). With Monte Blue*

*In THE GILDED HIGHWAY (1926).*

appeared as an unsympathetic wife in the comedy, *Beware of Married Men*. Loy followed with more vamp and "Oriental" bits. She was a native girl cast away on a South Sea island, this time with Walter Pidgeon in *Turn Back the Hours* (1928). For *Crimson City* (1928), she was transformed into an Oriental villainess. By this time, Loy had tired of her courtesan typecast—not just because she wanted more substantial roles but because all these evil ladies " . . . had to die in the end," as she told Chierichetti. "In *Crimson City*, I had to commit suicide by jumping off a ship off the coast of Santa Barbara in the middle of the night. Something went wrong, and I practically drowned."

Loy jitterbugged through a dance contest in Lloyd Bacon's *Pay as You Enter* (1928). Then Archie Mayo matched her again with Conrad Nagel, giving her the title role in *State Street Sadie* (1928). The complicated narrative begins with a bank employee's suicide after he is framed for a cop's murder. The man's brother, Ralph Blake (Nagel) enters, determined to uncover the real killer. Blake joins forces with Isabel (Loy), the dead cop's daughter, who disguises herself as State Street Sadie to avenge her father's murder. Together they discover the real killer, who leaps to his suicide from a skyscraper window. Blake and Sadie plan their wedding.

*The Midnight Taxi* (1928) followed *State Street Sadie* and found Loy hanging out with gangsters again—this time bootleggers who run their whiskey in a taxi fleet. This picture, which takes place mostly on a moving train, has a wild story. It involves stolen bonds, swiped jewelry, false arrest, and the hero's crazy chartered airplane ride back to the still moving train for the "revenge plot" dénouement. In all this, where is Myrna Loy? Lost in the night as a gangster's moll.

Loy was demoted to tenth billing for Michael Curtiz's *Noah's Ark*, not high enough for a reserved seat on Noah's chartered cruise. The picture opened on November 1, 1928 at Grauman's Chinese Theater, Loy's old stomping ground. She was dancing and vamping still—as "Dancer" in the film's modern segment and as "Slave Girl" in the Biblical portion. Cut to ninety-one minutes from its initial 141, the picture was re-released in 1957 with a new script and narration. As for the original, the reviews were mixed for Warners' attempt to create a film as spectacular as D. W. Griffith's *Intolerance*. *Variety* loved it; the *Los Angeles Times* hated it.

By 1929 Loy was back up to second billing behind Audrey Ferris in *Fancy Baggage*, yet another bootlegger's comedy. The same year Roy Del Ruth put together Warners' "First Vitaphone Operetta," *The Desert Song*, starring John Boles and Carlotta King. Del Ruth cast Loy as Azuri, a spurned "half-caste," who loves the man that Margot (King) plans to marry. But Margot really loves Pierre, the Red Shadow, who also loves Margot—a secret only Azuri knows. And so it goes. *The Desert Song* boasts camels, robes, women in skimpy, exotic outfits, masks, sand, a singing chorus of one hundred, and Myrna Loy, listed eighteenth in the credits.

John Ford saw *The Desert Song* and decided to have Fox Studio borrow her for the role of Yasmini, mystic enchantress and leader of a rebel Indian army in his production of *The Black Watch* (1929). Victor McLaglen shares top billing with Loy as Captain King, soldier in the Black Watch, who is sent on a special mission to India to keep Yasmini from leading her troops—"the fanatical hordes"—down the Khyber Pass.

Loy's Yasmini wears silk pants, a glittering halter top—which leaves her midriff bare and barely covers her breasts—and a bejeweled Egyptian headpiece (in India?). She resembles a weird cross between Cleopatra and the goddess Kali. Yasmini is a sensualist and a sadist—a passel of British soldiers are kept as slaves and whipped periodically at the guards'

*WHEN A MAN LOVES (1927). Myrna Loy at left*

*In SIMPLE SIS (1927)*

pleasure.

When Captain King visits in her bedroom, he finds her lounging seductively on a couch. He's about to ignore her overtures, but Yasmini reveals she's of Aryan blood—a white woman who is the descendant of Alexander the Great! Afterward, she sacrifices her life and her Indian conquests for love of King. He returns to Britain and the jovial comradeship of the Black Watch. Without the white woman to lead them, the now enfeebled hordes of India return peacefully to their homes. For a while, India is safe for British imperialist rule.

A side note: the first time Victor McLaglen pronounced Loy's film name, he uttered "Yes, Minnie," instead of Yasmini. The pronunciation was corrected for the final version, but not before Myrna Loy gained a nickname she has been stuck with ever since.

Back at Warners, Loy participated in the outrageous drama, *The Squall* (1929). Director Alexander Korda only remembered it as that "ghastly picture," the stupid story of a bushy-haired and baubled gypsy, Nubi (Loy), who takes shelter during a storm at a farmer's house and proceeds to whip all the vulnerable men into a sexual frenzy.

Nubi understands power through sex, rejecting one lover for any other of higher class—the servant for the son, the son for the father. She is a demon, Lilith reincarnated, tearing the house asunder. The men become cheats—violent liars, adulterers, withdrawn from their women (including Loretta Young). The son breaks his engagement and fails his college exams. Finally she is kicked out screaming while the whole gypsy tribe laughs at her and the film audience says, "Good riddance."

While the Korda film is monumentally laughable, with leaden lines and stage choreography, committed Loy fans can find their fun watching her vamp around, creating havoc in otherwise bland lives. Korda reported, "Many years later I reminded Myrna Loy of this adventure, and she said to me with a smile, 'That was a long time ago and I was then a child actress,' and I told her, most ungallantly, 'Yes, and I was a child director.' "

In *Hardboiled Rose* (1929), Loy is still another Southern belle, forced to work a gambling house to pay off her dead father's debts. In *Evidence* (1929) Loy plays a "native girl" again. And so it went, back and forth between occasional leads in second rank productions and tiny parts in major productions. The bouncing ball career of Myrna Loy, who was still more a starlet than a star, continued this way into the early thirties.

Warners' publicity program for *Show of Shows* (1929) bragged

*THE GIRL FROM CHICAGO (1927). With William Russell*

*CRIMSON CITY (1928). With Sojin*

*STATE STREET SADIE* (1928). With Conrad Nagel

about the movie's "seventy-seven stars and one thousand Hollywood beauties." These included Myrna Loy, who, somewhere between John Barrymore performing *Richard III* and a host of jazz numbers, danced and sang in "The Floradora Sextette."

In this number, Loy joins Alice Day, Lila Lee, Sally O'Neil, Patsy Ruth Miller and Marian Nixon, querying, "What's become of the Floradora Girls?" Loy is number three in the six-woman chorus line—the tallest of the bunch and the loveliest. None of the women, however, is very keen on keeping time. One steps a little ahead, another behind.

In the more successful "Chinese Fantasy" number, Loy, dressed as an Oriental, cavorts with Nick Lucas. The program introduces her by saying: "Myrna Loy specializes in exotic characterizations, although she is actually a native of Helena, Montana."

*Show of Shows* was typical of the big studio variety films that were popular around 1929 and 1930. The film companies took the opportunity to show off their contract talent and demonstrate the use of sound equipment. This par-

*THE DESERT SONG (1929). With John Boles*

*THE BLACK WATCH (1929). As Yasmini*

*THE SQUALL (1929). As Nubi*

*SHOW OF SHOWS (1929). The Floradora Sextet (left to right): Marian Nixon, Sally O'Neil, Myrna Loy, Patsy Ruth Miller, Lila Lee, and Alice Day*

ticular edition was directed by John Adolfi with "all dialogue and 86 percent color," and at the then outrageously steep cost of $800, 000.

Following *Show of Shows*, Loy was shoved back into her usual "native girl" routine. In fact, as Manuella, the Mexican servant in *The Great Divide* (1930), Loy sputters the same mock immigrant English used by Nubi in *The Squall*. Not only does Loy speak the old movie dialect, but she looks much the same—very alluring in Spanish gowns or low-cut peasant shirts and flowing skirts. She sports the hoop earrings again and a multitude of beads and bracelets around her neck and arms. She is also made up with lots of garish eye liner, and it's no wonder that Ruth (Dorothy Mackaill) looks annoyed when her Mexican rival dances before mine-owner Ghent (Ian Keith).

Manuella has an adolescent crush on Ghent. She's even trained his parakeet to chirp, "Just one kiss, Manuella," as she angles her hips and tilts her head close to give

THE GREAT DIVIDE (1930). With Ian Keith and Dorothy Mackaill

CAMEO KIRBY (1930). With George MacFarlane and J. Harold Murray

*UNDER A TEXAS MOON (1930). With Frank Fay*

Ghent the right idea. But he is a gentleman and thinks of her simply as the kid he watched grow up. Besides, she is Mexican; he is white—the racial distinction is important in this film based on the famous play by William Vaughn Moody.

In the end, Ruth and Ghent get together after he kidnaps her and carries her off into the hills. She falls in love with her abductor, while Loy's Manuella, without a mate, rides her pony alone into the First National sunset. Debutante Loy also gets dumped by her prince in the 1930 *Jazz Cinderella*.

Loy appeared as another tramp, Lea, paramour of an evil gambler, in the Fox film *Cameo Kirby* (1930). She was on loan for the third screen rendition of this Booth Tarkington story about New Orleans gambling during the Mardi Gras, 1850. There's a duel, a near-lynching and some good entertainment.

Back at Warners, Loy was stuck away on yet another South Seas island in *Isle of Escape* (1930). The jungle swarms with adventure, including a native uprising and a headhunting expedition. The white folks snub Loy, the native girl Moira, a beguiler out hunting Monte Blue, who prefers blonde Betty Compson.

Loy next played a woman beguiled by gay blade Frank Fay in Michael Curtiz's *Under a Texas Moon* (1930), a movie remembered more for the feud between star Fay and director Curtiz (in which Loy served as intermediary) than for any cinematic excellence. Despite the songs and dances and pretty scenery, the picture bored *Outlook and Independent's* Creighton Peet. The film critic reported fidgeting in his seat, "... counting lights in the theater ceiling and wishing I was in the Fiji islands or some other distant place."

Yet Peet intimated that, if he could steal away, he'd steal Myrna Loy away with him. While attacking Curtiz's photoplay, Peet raved about the fetching young actress, calling her Hollywood's only possible substitute for Garbo. He preached, "Give the girl a chance!" and continued with this early appreciation of Myrna Loy:

> It is true that Myrna Loy ... has never had a chance to do much of anything but run around in Oriental costumes and talk pidgin English .... Just because she is exotic and *mysteerious*, producers are afraid to give her a lead in a real picture. Years ago they said Garbo was too awkward to make a success on the screen—and now don't they look silly? Myrna Loy has intelligence and it is high time somebody gave her a decent part.

# GIVE THE GIRL A CHANCE

Someone at Sono-Art took notice of Myrna Loy. Her next film, *Cock O' the Walk* (1930), in which she played potentially the most complex role of her early career, was made on loan to that studio. In this screen adaptation of Arturo Mom's *Happiness Insurance*, director Walter Lang featured her as a suicide-prone lady married to gigolo Joseph Schildkraut. This callous opportunist had once saved Loy's life, before they tied the matrimonial knot. Afterward, he insures her and waits to collect on the premiums. Meanwhile he runs around with every married and misunderstood woman in town. When an irate husband tries to kill him, and Loy saves his life, the villainous spouse realizes, alas, he loves the wife left languishing in the background. The psychically frail Loy—sunken-eyed and with dark hair waving down her back, accentuating her smallness—there is more hair than person—grows suddenly irresistible to her wandering mate. But the intrigue continues, and the melodrama worsens.

A sleazy man links Loy's name to scandal, so hubby Schildkraut kills him, landing in prison and bringing Loy back to the brink of suicide. For a last time, he sincerely saves her, and with future happiness assured, Schildkraut returns for his brief prison stay. Critics had little good to say about this "meller," although the *New York Times* reviewer sat up from his otherwise languid notice to report, "Miss Loy acts her part exceptionally well. She has a pleasing voice . . . " And how did critic Creighton Peet feel about his love Loy's limp lead? "The whole thing made me feel pretty badly . . . His poor little wife-in-name-only is Myrna Loy, and the lines she has to speak must have been written by a new office boy who isn't quite on to things yet."

Loy returned to Warners for a supporting part as the sassy dancer, Sophie, in *Bride of the Regiment* (1930), a screen version of the operetta, *Lady in Ermine*. Her twirling atop tables was so inconsequential that *Variety* didn't even list her in their review. Warners then exiled her to Fox and Zane Grey's American West for a tiny role as bad man Bland's bad wife in *Last of the Duanes* (1930).

Next Loy flitted across the screen as Kara, "the Firefly," a hustling cabaret star in *The Truth About Youth* (1930). In her past, this gold digger ruined half a dozen young men with her "red hair and nude hips," according to co-star Loretta Young, who essentially repeats her Miss Pure Heart performance from *The Squall*.

Kara sings in a nightclub which

she also happens to own. To promote business for the club's opening, she plasters Lola-Lola-like posters all over town. She is displayed wearing a bikini and straddling an elephant, Western style, with the elephant's trunk pointed lewdly upward toward its rider. Unfortunately, the poster is more intriguing than the act—a failed pseudo-Dietrich routine. The chanteuse, photographed in long shot, seems to be mouthing her words, and her dance looks like a kindergarten ballet, clumsy and elephantine. When offstage, however, Loy brings humor and even a certain amount of integrity to her role. Despite her flirtations, her heart really belongs to only one sugar daddy. They enjoy a surprisingly mature relationship, including forgiving each other for sideline romances.

If *The Truth About Youth* was imitation *Blue Angel*, her next picture was ersatz *Morocco*. In *Renegades* (1930), Loy was back at Fox in exotic robes as the company mistress of a rebel army brigade comprised of dropouts from the regular French Legion. Warner Baxter has kidnapped her for being the spy that got him in trouble with the army. Loy pouts a lot, but she's undeniably intriguing as the woman doomed to be a camp follower—to run with

*COCK O' THE WALK (1930). With Joseph Schildkraut*

*THE TRUTH ABOUT YOUTH (1930). With David Manners*

the goats and the native women, even though she's "white." She even dares indulge in "the Secret Sin" of miscegenation, as she sleeps with the Arab commander as payment for freedom from Baxter. Her ultimate goal is power, female dominion over the Arab nations and command over all the legionnaires. She pays for her ambitions with her life, but not before taking nearly every member of the cast with her, including Baxter.

When she is shot and knows she's dying, she crawls across the subterranean desert, luring Baxter to her side with a smile, coaxing him closer for an embrace. Then she shoots him dead. His look of shock surpasses Kevin McCarthy's gulp of surprise when he discovers his lover has turned into a pod in *The Invasion of the Body Snatchers*. It's exciting and, yes, even funny, to watch Loy get revenge against the Legionnaires' Diseases of racism and sexism. Superficially, *Renegades* seems to revert back to Loy as trivial temptress. But for a modern audience, she does very well indeed.

Back to bits and vamps. Sono-

RENEGADES (1930).
As Eleanore

*THE NAUGHTY FLIRT (1931). With Paul Page and Alice White*

Art used Loy again as a clip joint's barfly in *Rogue of the Rio Grande* (1930). But much better, Samuel Goldwyn cast her as a blonde bewigged actress in *The Devil to Pay*. As Ronald Colman's mistress, she interferes with his plans to marry Loretta Young.

Loy began 1931 with *The Naughty Flirt*, in which one scene tells all we need to know of her hidden character: she wears a black chiffon evening dress, with arms flowing upright, almost from her waist, in the fashion of a bat. Although a soft-spoken debutante, Loy's Linda Gregory is no lady. She and brother Jack lost their sequined shirts in the stock market crash, and now they're after Alice White's millions. They hatch plots, from a bogus heart attack to a fraudulent love affair between Jack and Alice. But Alice White's friends save the day, pointing out her true boyfriend and pushing out Loy to poverty row.

Offscreen, Poverty Row became no joke for Myrna Loy. "Warners fired me," Loy later recalled. The benevolent Brothers failed to renew her lapsed five-year contract, and after all the movies she had given them. She was on the street again—with a fairly polished exotic accent and a string of already forgotten vamp movies behind her. Where to go with this strange

A CONNECTICUT YANKEE (1931). As Morgan Le Fay

*TRANSATLANTIC (1931). With Edmund Lowe*

cargo? To Fox, which signed Loy to a year's contract, and she promptly began her tenure as the heartless spy in the aerial melodrama, *Body and Soul* (1931), also a very early Bogart picture.

Whom next did she play? The egregious Morgan Le Fay. Will Rogers plays Hank, *A Connecticut Yankee* (1931), expert radio mechanic, who gets bonked on the head and transported back to Arthurian England. To save himself from a lynching, Hank calls forth an eclipse of the sun by uttering the magic words: "Prosperity, farm relief, freedom for Ireland, light wines and beer." Did Franklin Roosevelt model his winning 1932 platform on the wisdom of this Mark Twain hero? For this successful bit of sorcery, King Arthur knights Hank "Sir Boss" and he rejuvenates the King's court by installing service stations to oil and polish the knightly armor. Later he resorts to an old Will Rogers rodeo trick: he wins a jousting match by lassoing his opponent.

Watching the action from the side is Morgan Le Fay, the King's sister, who licks her lips and prepares her seduction. Honorable Hank rejects Morgan's advances and frees all her captives, so she decides to hang him. She ties him on the scaffold, with no hope of an

*REBOUND (1931). With Robert Ames*

eclipse to save him again. Each drop of her hand signifies the execution of another "poor knave," and Hank's death draws nearer—until five hundred tiny tanks, helicopters, planes and Austins come to his rescue. Morgan Le Fay chases Hank with a dagger, but he awakens from his dream before she catches him.

Heinous Morgan Le Fay, one of Loy's nastiest screen characterizations, also turns out to be an exponent of gallows humor. Everyone knows that Hank won't get his neck stretched, so it's just for fun that the pokey cowboy, lost in Connecticut and then lost in Arthurian England, is chased around by Loy's Miss Le Fay. Her next movie was not much. In *Hush Money* (1931), she was lost as an insignificant member of a bandit brood. Joan Bennett was starred as a crooked girl who eventually goes straight.

William K. Howard's ambitious shipboard murder mystery, *Transatlantic* (1931) was a kind of floating pre- *Grand Hotel*. Failed banks and burglaries are stirred together with individual traumas of failed marriages and dead-end love affairs. Among other intrigues, banker John Halliday abandons his long-suffering wife, Myrna

*CONSOLATION MARRIAGE (1931). As Elaine*

*ARROWSMITH (1931). With Ronald Colman*

Loy, for the jazzy Greta Nissen. Director Howard allowed Loy sympathetic sides to her characterization far away from her wicked woman roles. When Halliday, jilted by Nissen, returns to his anguished wife, she accepts him with unquestioning grace—the wisdom of an older Loy, never realized before in the movies.

Moving back to shore, Loy embarked at RKO studio for *Rebound* (1931) as a vile little homewrecker. Reportedly, when director Edward H. Griffith tested Loy for the "other woman" part, star Ina Claire cracked, "That girl couldn't take a man away from me!" But since no appropriate performer could be found by the shooting date, Loy went into the part. And she was just fine. No question, this slinky Loy could steal anyone.

In *Rebound*, Loy is bored, bad, and beautiful; all she has to do is bend her little finger and Robert Ames comes running—beginning his extramarital affair at the most inelegant time, during his honeymoon with Ina. Ames brings Loy to his honeymoon hotel suite. Thus, Claire discovers that not only does she share her man, bad enough, but worse, she and Loy even wear the same dress. "What a washout you turned out to be," she tells her hubby, who continues messing openly with his lover. They sip champagne at the ocean until the inevitable shakedown —after which husband and wife reunite.

After a single film at Fox—*Skyline* (1931), in which Loy stands about as architect Thomas Meighan's flame—she returned to her other woman status in *Consolation Marriage* (1931) at RKO. Pat O'Brien, her former childhood sweetheart, whom she has jilted, marries Irene Dunne on the rebound. But boredom with her own life brings Myrna back into his life, and O'Brien, like Robert Ames before him, awaits her with bated breath. When Loy returns to pick up her man, Dunne steps aside with masochistic solicitude. Nevertheless, she can be heard sighing happily a mile away, when O'Brien shows Loy the gate.

At about this time, Fox also gave Myrna Loy her walking papers with the lapse of her one-year contract. But 1931 didn't close so badly. John Ford cast her as the tender Joyce Lanyon in Samuel Goldwyn's production of *Arrowsmith*.

Ford's *Arrowsmith* brought good fortune into Loy's life. Not that she had a tremendous part—in fact, most reviews of the film ignored her entirely. But wonderful things happened to her on that set. Arthur Hornblow, Jr. hung around quite a lot for an assistant producer. He was smitten by the young Montana beauty—and they were to marry five years later.

More good fortune occurred. MGM's "boy wonder" producer, Irving Thalberg, had spotted Loy in *Skyline* and added her name to the glamorous cast of stars under his studio's moniker. Loy now was only a hop, skip and jump—a song and dance, a *Wet Parade* and a *Prizefighter and the Lady*—away from superstardom.

Myrna Loy's metamorphosis from rotten tomato to angel cake happened neither suddenly nor magically after she crossed the threshold into MGM. She continued paying her dues, with long hours whiled away and wasted, still as village vamp and hard-boiled hussy. As an actress, Loy learned to be better by being even "badder." To add dimension to her basic Third World enchantress, Loy says she "read Oriental philosophy and tried to steep myself in Oriental thinking. I didn't know then how difficult it would be to break away from the type I was perfecting."

Opening her career at Metro, Loy played Isabel, the malicious older daughter, in Clarence Brown's *Emma* (1932). Marie Dressler is Emma, nanny and maternal figure to the four motherless Smith children. The picture begins in 1911, with Mrs. Smith dying in childbirth, and Emma spanking life into the barely breathing baby, Ronnie, while the other children run around, squeal, fight and shout for their nanny. Twenty years later—1931—the children, grown up and rich from their daddy's scientific inventions, still demand their nanny. These kids are now a pack of fools, snobby and selfish, with the oldest, Isabel (Loy), insisting that Emma wear a maid's cap while serving meals.

# MYRNA'S MISCELLANEA

The father disgraces his snotty scions by marrying the servant Emma, and he wills the good and loyal woman his whole fortune. When daddy dies, Isabel drags Emma to court, claiming the old man was poisoned by his new wife. Everyone, including judge and jury, sees through the shameful accusation. When Emma is declared innocent, she punishes the children most cruelly by moving out on them. Over Isabel's sudden tears of remorse, Emma heads off to care for a new family in New Jersey. Yet another infant will be saved by the big, ugly, saintly woman.

Was there anything new in the role of Isabel above the demeaning parts played by Loy at Warners, Fox and Sono-Art? She felt not, and the nasty typecast depressed her. Loy moped about the *Emma* set for days until brusque Emma, Marie Dressler herself, straightened things out. Dressler barked, "Get your chin up, kid. You've got the whole world ahead of you. Lord bless you, what do you expect to be—a star when you start?"

Everyone around chuckled, and Loy laughed at herself, too. She was grateful that Marie Dressler, a top box-office star, would stop to remind her to be patient. Myrna Loy said of Dressler, "The millions

*EMMA (1932). With Marie Dressler and George Meeker*

who have heard her infectious laugh will understand how much it meant to me that day."

For Victor Fleming's mishap, *The Wet Parade* (1932), a confused shambles of Upton Sinclair's fire-and-brimstone, pro-Prohibition novel, Loy held her chin up and sported a blonde wig. All this was for a drunken bit as a selfish jazz-age dame who foresakes her boyfriend when he is blinded by rot-gut whiskey.

Irving Thalberg loaned her to an independent, Allied Pictures, for a modern mock-up of Thackeray's *Vanity Fair* (1932). (The head of the studio, M. H. Hoffman, was a sucker for literary classics, so he decided to make them in cheap "B" form. Allied's *Unholy Love*, for example, was a tinsel version of *Madame Bovary*, and sat right next to the company's Hoot Gibson Westerns.) Nobody noticed Myrna Loy's brave attempt at a budget Becky Sharp. Before returning to Metro, she passed again through Fox, appearing as Sari Lodar, questioned for the murder of a dashing concert singer, in *The Woman in Room 13* (1932), an unlucky picture. Home to Metro, where Myrna played Myra in the

*THE WET PARADE (1932). With Neil Hamilton*

Paris-set *New Morals For Old* (1932), "a case of parents will be parents and youth in the twenties will be headstrong," according to the *New York Times* critic, exasperated by yet another indifferent "generation gap" saga.

Rouben Mamoulian gave Myrna Loy a much more impressive part in the superb musical comedy, *Love Me Tonight* (1932), arguably the first "classic" movie in which the actress appeared. Alongside major stars Maurice Chevalier and Jeanette MacDonald, she was cast as the completely man-crazy Countess Valentine. Paramount didn't want her, and Loy didn't think she could play the part. "But Rouben insisted," Loy confided to David Chierichetti. "The part of Valentine didn't even exist in the script. I was given my lines every morning, typed on blue interoffice memo paper, and we worked them into the script."

Among these improvisations was this famous tasty exchange:

*Jeanette*: "Don't you ever think of anything but men, dear?"

*Myrna*: "Oh yes!"

*Jeanette*: "Oh, of what?"

*NEW MORALS FOR OLD (1932). With Robert Young*

*Myrna*: "Of schoolboys."

Maestro Mamoulian choreographed elaborate, tantalizing numbers to decorate his operatic parody of a tailor in love with a princess. Several slightly naughty scenes led to a painful slashing of footage in the fifties by the censors, including Loy's "moment of truth" in the "Mimi" montage. As she describes it, she was spliced out because the Countess wore a "very transparent nightgown, and when I got out of bed, my navel showed."

The Countess's riveting bare belly still could not equal the hypnotic power of Ursula Georgi, Loy's multinational killer in *Thirteen Women* (1932) at RKO. Her scheme is mass murder by "autosuggestion," ridding the world of twelve sorority sisters who scorned her on racial grounds, causing the half-Javanese, half-Indian Ursula to drop out of college. Her plan is to drive the dozen chums to emotional collapse and then suicide by tampering with the horoscope readings of Swami Yogadachi. Little do these women realize that their happy charts have been rewritten to predict doom.

Irene Dunne, the levelheaded leader of the group, doesn't believe in horoscopes. Ursula attempts to do away with Irene by way of her son, planting bombs in his toys and poison in his candy.

*LOVE ME TONIGHT (1932). With Maurice Chevalier and Jeanette MacDonald*

*THIRTEEN WOMEN (1932). With Edward Pawley*

*THE MASK OF FU MANCHU (1932). With Charles Starrett*

When Dunne demands to know why she torments her, Ursula explains what it means to be "a half breed in a world ruled by whites. If you're a male, you're a coolie. If you're female, you're a . . . The only way I could flee myself was by becoming white." Never mind the potential seriousness of the political commentary. No one likes a child molester, so the one-woman guerrilla warfare ends as Ursula falls off the rear of the train—just as her boyfriend, the late Swami, had predicted.

The racist association of dark skin with perverse sexuality and violence carried over to *The Mask of Fu Manchu* (1932), in which Loy plays the lascivious Fah Lo See, daughter of Sax Rohmer's famous madman scientist and Harvard graduate. In this adventure, Fu Manchu (Boris Karloff) seeks world domination with the aid of Genghis Khan's mask and sword. Loy wears long exotic robes, dazzling jewels in her hair, and goes glassy-eyed with tremulous excitement when her servants lash at the hero, Terrence (Charles Starrett).

The movie does nothing to conceal its *Birth of a Nation* attitudes—white supremacy over the "barbaric yellow races," waspish puritanism pitted against the decadence of Fu Manchu and his followers. Loy and Karloff play their parts with wicked tongue-in-cheek humor that makes the film amusing as a half-conscious satire of imperialist genre pictures. "That part was quite unactable," Loy recalled of Miss Manchu. "I had just discovered Freud . . . and was appalled to find that not only was I supposed to have a pet python but that I used to have my father's male victims turned over to me for torture, stripped. I then whipped them myself, uttering sadistic, gleeful cries."

How did she survive the trauma? "I became quite friendly with the python," Myrna Loy said. As for her inane role, "I've never lived it down and my friend Roddy McDowall calls me 'Fu' to this day."

It was around this time that Irving Thalberg called Myrna Loy into his executive office for a heart-to-heart. He told her that she had star quality, "but there is something holding you back . . . there seems to be a veil between you and the audience. You've got to cut through. You must reach out there and grab them!" Loy followed the advice religiously, fighting her small-town timidity, working to become more gregarious. "I had to

*THE ANIMAL KINGDOM (1932). With William Gargan and Leslie Howard*

*TOPAZE (1933). With Frank Reicher, John Barrymore, and Albert Conti*

get over that," Loy commented in a 1933 interview, "I was suffering too much."

Loy's problems were coming to an end. Director Edward Griffith remembered the woman who stole Ina Claire's husband in *Rebound* and gave her the sensational role of Cecilia in his film version of the Philip Barry play, *The Animal Kingdom*. Two stories circulate about Griffith's choice of Loy. In *Memo from David O. Selznick*, the producer pats himself on the back for wisely approving Griffith's casting: "Myrna Loy had been playing Oriental sirens for years . . . It was considered a revolutionary thing to put her in a polite comedy such as *The Animal Kingdom*, but when this casting was suggested to me by Griffith, the director, I leaped at the idea." Loy tells a slightly different version of the RKO "revolution." Her tale involves sneaking about and testing at odd hours of the night because "David Selznick was adamant; he wanted Karen Morley as Leslie Howard's wife and wouldn't even let Ned test me."

The screen test went well, except that Loy devoured Mexican sausage for lunch while studying

THE BARBARIAN (1933). With Ramon Novarro

her part, which repulsed her vegetarian leading man, Leslie Howard. Afterward, Loy stuck to rice pudding, and, because of the eventual critical success of *Animal Kingdom*, RKO stuck with her for the role of the mistress in *Topaze* (1933).

Director Harry D'Arrast's *Topaze* opens on Myrna Loy's Coco, a luscious, lazy lady, surrounded by Art Deco objects, drinking martinis, smoking cigarettes, and conversing on the phone. "Who is your son's tutor?" she asks the Baron who keeps her. "Topaze!" replies the Baron, who is soon scurrying home to his legal mate. Coco, a tolerant mistress abandoned once too often, becomes a ripe romantic target for Topaze, handsome John Barrymore.

Topaze sports a craggy beard and slipping glasses, and his too long, barely combed hair flops down toward a scarf flung gingerly around his neck. Dizzy and discomfitted among the upper classes, Topaze would really prefer to live at ease, a spiritual innocent among his schoolboys. Instead he is fired for flunking the Baron's son and is then hired by the Baron to perfect "Bubbling Topaze," a school kids' soft drink which also possesses strange and magical powers.

Coco steps in to help the schoolmarmish inventor cope with the material world and to guide him

*THE PRIZEFIGHTER AND THE LADY (1933). With Walter Huston*

toward "manhood." The twosome go to the movies, fall in love, and stay out all night. When Bubbling Topaze grows into a business empire, Topaze himself is transformed into a slick, nattily dressed capitalist entrepeneur.

The expected fall from grace for Topaze never occurs. He gets his cake and eats it too, keeping his money and winning Coco. Loy's Coco is an ambivalent figure. She feels badly about Topaze's lost innocence, yet she is pleased to see him develop into such a breadwinner. In this movie, money means sexuality, and Topaze just gets sexier and sexier.

Coco represents the iconoclastic flaunting of traditional values. She is both vamp and sophisticate. She can drink with the boys, cheat like the rich, but basically she's down-to-earth, a good egg. (Nora Charles is just around the corner.)

MGM must have been embarrassed. Lowly RKO had twice borrowed their contract player, Myrna Loy, and scored back-to-back critical successes with *The Animal Kingdom* and *Topaze*. For their own part, MGM could come up with nothing better than *The Barbarian* (1933), in which Loy, as an American of Egyptian origin, is sung to by Ramon Novarro. The silent star of *Ben-Hur* was past his prime in the talkies, and Loy, who had been relegated to the most minor role in *Ben-Hur*, was now biding time while Novarro crooned "Love Song of the Nile" in this "grandson of the sheik" costume pageant.

Meanwhile MGM ordered a special script called *The Sailor and the Lady* from their crackerjack scenarist, Francis Marion, especially patented for Clark Gable and Myrna Loy. When the studio bosses learned that Gable wasn't available, they replaced him with boxer Max Baer, fresh from his ring victory over Max Schmeling, and renamed the picture *The Prizefighter and the Lady* (1933). The switch infuriated Francis Marion, who complained, "Gene Tunney is my friend. He married a beautiful society girl—and they might think I have exploited their love affair. You can't do this." Director Howard Hawks, who initially was contracted to direct the film, was angry for different reasons: "They cast it with Max Baer and Myrna Loy—complete opposites. In other words, Max Baer was the stooge and Loy was the lady. I said 'I don't want to make the picture.' And they said, 'Will you help out, do a couple of weeks' work, give Baer a start, teach him a little about acting? Then Woody Van Dyke will take over.' I said sure."

Whatever the behind-the-screen story, Max Baer's surprise talent won all the publicity for this picture. The rave reviews ignored even the grand Walter Huston as the

*WHEN LADIES MEET (1933). With Ann Harding and Alice Brady*

pugilist's trainer, "the Professor," not to mention the "stooge's" haughty lady, nightclub queen Myrna Loy.

After winning her rugged Samson, Max Baer, in *The Prizefighter and the Lady*, Myrna Loy joined forces with Ann Harding to sort out their errant love lives in *When Ladies Meet* (1933). Loy plays a *professional*, a novelist, stuck on her publisher, Frank Morgan. Inadvertently, she meets the man's wife (Harding), who gives her some common sense advice about straying husbands. Loy settles for journalist Robert Montgomery. The film of Rachel Crothers' play is a decent but unmemorable excursion into romantic drama. Its virtues and faults are well summarized by Mordaunt Hall's *New York Times* critique: "It is an intelligent and amusing production, even though as a film it is somewhat long on words and short on drama."

Director Woody Van Dyke had liked Myrna Loy in *The Prizefighter and the Lady*. Within

*PENTHOUSE (1933). With Warner Baxter*

several months, he put her back to work as Gertie, the almost angelic moll in *Penthouse* (1933). With the same female star (Loy), same scriptwriters (Albert Hackett and Frances Goodrich), same director (Van Dyke), everything in this gangster drama looks ahead to the next year's adaptation of Dashiell Hammett's *The Thin Man*—except a leading man and a dog!

Blood and gore ooze through *Penthouse*. Sadistic cops threaten to throw a mobster out a window unless he squeals, then the good gangster dies happily with blood gushing from his mouth while Warner Baxter lovingly recites his vile characteristics in eulogy. Meanwhile, Gertie, with humble self-deprecation, risks her life again and again for her man, Warner Baxter. "Your life is just a little more important than mine," she tells him.

Baxter plays a rich attorney, Jackson Durrant, who has taken to defending falsely accused racketeers and con men to the chagrin of his properly placed, upper-class

A portrait in the early thirties

fiancée (Mae Clarke). Finally, she engages herself to another rich boy who, in turn, must be rid of his mistress. Someone bumps her off. Durrant must discover "who done it" and save the boyfriend from the hot seat. Gertie helps him. She also helps him learn that all women aren't temptresses.

In every way, the two women in *Penthouse* are different—one has official class, the other is classy. They both define themselves in terms of their men—Mae Clarke can't make a move without being engaged to someone—but while Loy is fastidiously faithful, Clarke is fashionably faithless. The distinctions between the women are paralleled in male behavior. The "good" gangsters are the low-life types, while the "bad" ones move with respectable society and live in penthouse apartments. The movie asserts that morality is dependent on class—that the working class has a stronger moral code. Interestingly, this is not unlike the Charles's discovery in the *Thin Man* series that murder and crime move hand in hand with wealth. A strange but revealing theme for mighty and wealthy Metro-Goldwyn-Mayer!

# THE KING, HIS FORGOTTEN QUEEN, AND THE NEW PRINCE

Movie fans today know Myrna Loy above all as William Powell's "perfect wife"—the cheeky woman who palled around with Asta and assorted crooks in *The Thin Man* adventures. But before getting there, as Powell's wife, Loy enjoyed quite a fling as Clark Gable's girl.

No one forgets Gable's title, "King of Hollywood" but few recall that Minnie from Montana shared the throne as filmdom's Queen. By the time Ed Sullivan officially crowned the royal pair in 1936 as "King and Queen of Hollywood," Loy and Gable had co-starred seven times. While linking Gable's name to Crawford, Harlow, Turner, and, of course, Vivien Leigh, no film historian mentions Loy as one of Gable's major screen loves. For the record, Gable romanced Crawford eight times, Harlow enjoyed six love matches, and Turner fell for Gable a mere four times. But perhaps to write about the amorous linking of Gable and Loy seems, to *Thin Man* zealots, tantamount to accusing the perfect wife of adultery!

Gable and Loy's reign began in 1933 with *Night Flight*, a Clarence Brown cinematization of Antoine de Saint-Exupery's poetic novel of heroic mail pilots. John Barrymore played Riviere, boss of the Buenos Aires air crew. In a fashion similar to Cary Grant in Howard Hawks's later *Only Angels Have Wings*, the unyielding flight commander orders takeoffs without concern for safety, disregarding the lack of night lights or impossible weather conditions. His hard line leads to pilot Gable's death as well as that of Loy's Brazilian pilot husband (William Gargan). *The New York Times* called *Night Flight* "probably the most authentic flying story that has come to the screen." Clarence Brown maintained the ironic theme of wasted bravery from Saint-Exupery: "Flying in the dark is risking the lives of pilots just to give somebody in Paris the satisfaction of receiving a post on Tuesday instead of Thursday."

Loy and Gable were together again in the metropolitan hospital which housed the *Men in White* (1934). (In typical sumptuous MGM fashion, the hospital looks to be a lavish Art Deco replica of Rockefeller Center.) Dr. George Ferguson (Gable) has pushed his way up from the slums to work as a medical practitioner in this screen version of Sidney Kingsley's "realistic" but creaky Broadway drama. Despite his lowly intern's status, Ferguson proves indispensable. He's on call *willingly*

*NIGHT FLIGHT (1933). With William Gargan*

twenty-four hours a day, to the everlasting dismay of his fiancée, Laura Hudson, played by Myrna Loy. A spoiled heiress (Laura's financier father supports the hospital), Laura devotes her life to nothing except social gatherings and Gable. She resents his late night working, for she cannot imagine any other existence than her own trivial, self-absorbed lifestyle.

Laura's education comes when Ferguson, temporarily deserted by this lady, spends the night with nurse Barbara (Elizabeth Allan), who had swooned when he saved a child's life. Barbara gets pregnant and has a far-off-screen abortion resulting in a terminal case of peritonitis. Before her illness, Ferguson was prepared to forsake his serious studies to marry Laura and take a cushy hospital job. But Barbara's critical condition reminds him of his duty: he must operate!

Head physician Hochberg (Jean Hersholt) invites Laura to watch Barbara's operation, and Laura does everything wrong: she jokes about the dumpy surgical gown, touches Ferguson's arm after he's

*MEN IN WHITE (1934). With Clark Gable*

been sterilized, and, most vulgar of all, faints the minute the cutting begins. Barbara meets Laura briefly but dies holding Ferguson's hand. Her head slips slowly out of the frame, leaving visible only a crucifix created from shadows on the window. The sign of the cross: hope for the future. George returns to round-the-clock medicine and serious study. As for Laura? Perhaps she'll leave George alone and quit nagging the old workhorse to go dancing.

Otis Ferguson commented in *The New Republic* that "Clark Gable and Myrna Loy, nice people in any situation, didn't get very strong parts," in *Men in White*. In fact, their parts were too strong, bombastic and exaggerated. The strident Loy role painfully documents the implied misogyny in the conception of many so-called "independent" women in Hollywood pictures. Such women are spoiled, insensitive, and brash, but really weaklings who faint at the moment of any genuine trouble. Still they persist in rebelling against their appropriate niches in society—as understanding, supportive wives, and as helpmates—like the nurses aiding the noble male doctors.

The story of *Men in White* is so silly that only an AMA convention today could appreciate it. Kingsley's play made prime parody material for one of *Your Show of Shows*' most inspired comedy sketches on television. Sid Caesar, as the madly idealistic intern, recites the Hippocratic Oath about a dozen times, driving everyone to distraction. (In this sketch, Pat Crowley played the Myrna Loy part.)

Audiences remember the 1934 *Manhattan Melodrama* for all sorts of reasons, but mostly because the movie was bait, used by the Lady in Red to lure gangster John Dillinger to his death. More historical gore—the film's opening sequence of a boating disaster was taken from an actual event, the 1904 burning of the *General Slocum*, considered the worst maritime disaster of its time, killing hundreds of women and children on a Sunday outing sponsored by the Lutheran Church. On the sunny side—*Manhattan Melodrama* was the occasion for the all-important screen introduction of William Powell to Myrna Loy.

Two kids orphaned on the *General Slocum* are Blackie Gallagher and Jim Wade, soon grown up as Clark Gable and William Powell, respectively. Jim makes it in the law, as an attorney. Blackie makes it in spite of the law, as a hustling gambler and racketeer, whose girl Eleanor (Myrna Loy) cautions him that "You'll win somebody's mother some night."

Blackie and Jim meet up again at the fight of Dempsey vs. Firpo.

*MEN IN WHITE (1934). With Jean Hersholt*

*MANHATTAN MELODRAMA (1934). With William Powell*

Myrna Loy in 1934

Jim, running for District Attorney, invites Blackie to a victory party. When Blackie can't go, he sends Eleanor instead. She barges through a cheering crowd, leaps into Jim's taxi and falls on his lap and in love with the proper-speaking gent, who spends the night telling Eleanor his life story ("I was born at home because I wanted to be near mother"). The hip Eleanor, sophisticated lady of the gambler's world, switches allegiance from law breaker Blackie to law enforcer Jim, who represents security, polite comfort, and attentive loving. "Maybe it's very out of style," Eleanor explains to Blackie. "Maybe I want to wear last year's hat." Also, Jim does not kiss her after their first meeting, and that impresses Eleanor.

Eleanor and Jim marry with Blackie's blessings, but the camaraderie runs into trouble when Blackie kills Jim's political rival. Jim, more faithful to the code of law than the code of friendship, acts as prosecuting attorney at Blackie's trial, securing the governorship on his friend's conviction. Blackie goes to the electric chair.

While *Manhattan Melodrama* concentrates more on the relationship between the men than on Eleanor, Loy's presence asserts itself dynamically as the mediator between the estranged childhood chums, virtuous Jim and the knightly killer Blackie. As the *New York Post* critic wrote, Loy brought "charm and persuasive dignity to the role of the girl. Her performance confirms the conviction that Myrna Loy is one of the screen's most intelligent and personable players."

A publicity photo for the film shows the three stars together, with Loy hanging her arm around Gable and yet leaning toward Powell. Gable looks amused, but he is outside the romantic sphere generated by the other two. Loy already gravitates toward Powell. With Gable, Loy's more passive, introverted side was most often in evidence under the onslaught of his aggressive, he-man characterizations. But Powell was too genial and mannerly and much too self-confident to need to be overpowering. His light cat-dancing style left room for Loy to breathe. She could be quiet and serious when she wanted, but she also could emerge at other times as a modern woman—clever, witty, social, competent. At such moments, she even seemed to grow taller.

Between Gable and Loy, there was interesting interaction, but with Powell and Loy there were those special vibrations. "From the very first scene we did together in *Manhattan Melodrama*," Loy has confided, "we felt that particular magic there was between us."

## THE THIN MAN

After exercising Myrna Loy's evil, vampish persona for good with *Manhattan Melodrama*, director Woody Van Dyke teamed her a second time with William Powell in *The Thin Man* (1934), thus forming Hollywood's most tantalizing detective duo, Nick and Nora Charles. But Metro magnate Louis B. Mayer grumbled over the assignment of Loy and Powell to the Charles's role. He thought them dull, not droll. Clearly he could not have been more shortsighted. From their first moments together on screen, they matched magnificently, moving in sublime synchronization. "There was this feeling of rhythm, of complete understanding, and an instinct of how each of us could bring out the best in the other," Loy recalls of her partnership with Powell.

Van Dyke was known as the "one take" director, "One Shot Woody," sometimes to the detriment of his craft. But as critic Andrew Sarris notes, "Perhaps carelessness and haste are precisely the qualities responsible for the breezy charm of . . . *The Thin Man*." Van Dyke shot *The Thin Man* in a typical (for him) twelve days. This speedup meant that the slightest suggestion or improvisation might be taken seriously and incorporated into the film. Loy described one such incident in a *New York Times* interview: "I had to make an entrance into the hotel where Nick Charles was drinking . . . Our dog Asta . . . was on the end of the leash. Well, he recognized Bill, and dragged me over the threshold —sprawling—so Woody decided to go one better, and shoot the scene with Nora bundled up with parcels after shopping."

Loy's tumble transformed into one of the greatest slapstick entrances in film. Loy is yanked onto the scene, dragged bodily behind Asta. She pulls frantically on his leash and flops finally on a tavern floor in front of the terrier's master, suave Nick, who stands nonchalantly by, sipping scotch and downing doubles. Nora begins catching up with Nick's sousing. But murder interrupts their bacchanal and sends Nick and Nora prowling basements and bars in search of Clyde Wynant, accused assassin, whose mangled torso soon appears before the real slayer tips his hand.

Nick and Nora are a lovely pair of lunatics. Nick is pathologically lazy, living proudly off his wealthy wife. But Nora's sheltered, aristocratic background makes her thrill-hungry. She loves meeting Nick's low-life pals, the bookies, cops and cons with whom he once cavorted. Nora constantly coaxes Nick into taking her to wrestling matches or becoming entwined in complicated mysteries he would more

*THE THIN MAN (1934). With William Powell and Asta*

happily ignore. As the ever-so-slightly slighted female, Nora sometimes realizes adventures only vicariously, arriving at the tail end of Nick's escapades. But she is shrewd and smart, so Nora's involvement is not often simply back seat.

Under the protective umbrella of a respectable, upper-class marriage, Nick and Nora share the fun of fast living—a lifestyle usually reserved in the cinema for singles. They are partygoers and steady imbibers, but Nick and Nora drink together and go home together. Despite banter about infidelity and promiscuity, Nick and Nora enjoy a lusciously sensuous but definitely monogamous relationship. Even in non-*Thin Man* films, except for an occasional flirtation (such as in *Evelyn Prentice* and *Love Crazy*), the Powell-Loy dual personae is one of constancy. They are the perfect couple in the perfect marriage. They did the outrageous—they enjoyed each other as man and wife.

*The Thin Man* detective film crept close to screwball comedy, with the Charles's bickering and bantering like a couple of mad hatter Capra characters. (Interestingly, Frank Capra wanted Loy for *It Happened One Night*, but she turned down the part of heiress Ellie Andrews.) When Nora sends

Nick off on the dangerous mission, she sidles up close to her hubby as if to make love, then purrs comically, "I think it's a dirty trick to bring me all the way to New York just to make a widow out of me." "You wouldn't be a widow long," he retorts. "Not with all your money!"

Van Dyke's movie was based on the Dashiell Hammett novel, *The Thin Man*, a book dedicated to the hardboiled author's lover for thirty years before his death, Lillian Hellman, who was the real-life model for Nora. When they met, she was twenty-four and he was thirty-six and just getting done with a week-long drunk. Hellman writes, "He . . . was the hottest thing in Hollywood and New York." He was an ex-Pinkerton man with marks on his body from scrapes with the criminal element. However, he was also "gentle in manner, well-educated, elegant to look at, born of early settlers, was eccentric, witty and spent so much money on women that they would have liked him even if he had been none of the good things."

If he sounds like the mustachioed, dimple-cheeked Powell, it is no accident. And in fact, the film couple's lovable jokester relationship is captured in this

*THE THIN MAN (1934). With Maureen O'Sullivan, Henry Wadsworth, William Powell, and Asta*

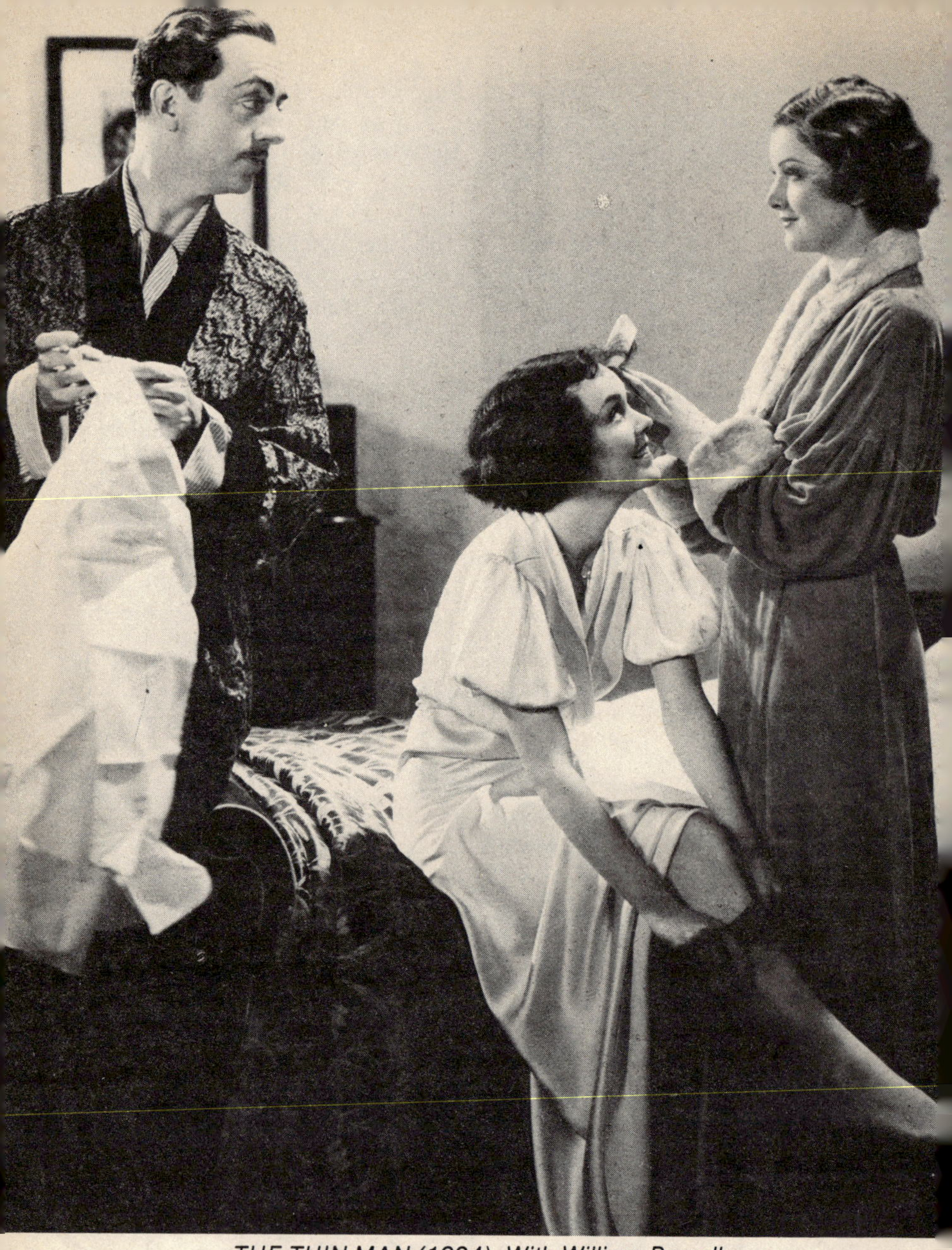

*THE THIN MAN (1934). With William Powell and Maureen O'Sullivan*

interchange between Hammett and his playwright amour, Hellman: "For years we made jokes about the day I would write about him . . . 'Tell me more about the girl in San Francisco. The silly one who lived across the hall in Pine Street.' And he would laugh and say, 'She lived across the hall in Pine Street and was silly.' "

By the time Loy appeared in *The Thin Man*, her career was almost two-thirds behind her—about seventy-seven films had passed. Yet, as Loy claims, "the picture made me—and it inspired the press. From that time on I was typed as the perfect wife." She became "instantly" one of Metro's major properties and Hollywood's hottest stars.

As Loy describes her beloved characterization: "Nora of *The Thin Man* was different . . . Nora had a gorgeous sense of humor; she appreciated the distinctive grace of her husband's wit. She laughed . . . at and with him when he was funny. What's more, she laughed at herself. Besides having tolerance, she was a good guy. She was courageous and interested in living and she enjoyed all the things she did. You understand, she had a good time, always."

Between Powell and Loy's performance in *The Thin Man* and their subsequent work in *Evelyn Prentice* a few months later, the actress spied as Fraulein Doctor in Sam Wood's *Stamboul Quest* (1934). As a World War I German espionage agent, Loy spends her time ducking romance with American George Brent, who, ignorant of her professional duties, has followed her to Constantinople. While dealing with Brent, the lady spy simultaneously attempts to discover if the Turkish commander, Ali Bey, is leaking information to the allies.

For her spying, Loy depends much less on her sexual wiles and much more on her intelligence, which led to praise from *The New York Times*: "She does not go around, as have so many other such heroines, with so obviously an air of mystery . . . Miss Loy is an actress—and that, after all, is really not new."

Myrna Loy and William Powell were paired for the third time in 1934 in *Evelyn Prentice*, directed by Loy's *Transatlantic* friend, veteran William K. Howard. Evelyn Prentice (Loy) enjoys the leisure life of class and wealth, Park Avenue and mink, luncheon at the Waldorf, tea at the Plaza. But she is also lonely. Despite the appearance of a contented marriage, she has an attorney husband, John (William Powell) who attends to clients

## THE PERFECT WIFE

more than his family. In *Evelyn Prentice*, Powell and Loy are *not* the perfect couple.

While tucking her daughter in bed at night, she hears the child murmur, "Mommy, why do I always kiss you for Daddy?" Too many solo cocktail hours make Evelyn prey for cads such as Lawrence Kennard (Harvey Stephens). He's a smooth-talking poet of hearts-and-flowers verse—a would-be playwright out to find a rich dame, a black fur "angel" who will pump money into his play. When he spots Evelyn at an uptown cafe—manless and sober—he thinks he's found her. He sends her poetry and bouquets while John's away, but Evelyn remains loyal, until . . .

She discovers that John has been traveling with a former client—manhunter Nancy Harrison, whom he defended on a manslaughter charge (Rosalind Russell, in her first screen role). He denies the nasty implications, yet the grim situation sends Evelyn to Kennard long enough for him to blackmail her.

Loy threatens Kennard with his own gun, and when he is actually murdered—shot through the heart by his heartbroken mistress —Evelyn mistakenly thinks she did it. Despite massive mistaken identities, the murder is solved. At the

*STAMBOUL QUEST (1934). With Rudolph Amendt and George Brent*

baby's bed, the Prentice couple are reunited, just when Evelyn thought herself too utterly disgraced to ever face John again. The ending is reminiscent of *Blonde Venus*'s close, but improving on the Sternberg picture, the husband does not need to forgive the wife. Both the Prentices acted stupidly and are prepared to face each other squarely as Nick-and-Nora, Loy-and-Powell equals.

(Actually the great scene of *Evelyn Prentice* is an earlier moment, a temporary reconciliation. John Prentice walks in to the apartment while Evelyn and their daughter are exercising. He joins the calisthenics. The three lie on the floor, lifting limbs, groaning and counting, and the adults patch up their quarrel.)

Although Loy had rejected Frank Capra's invitation to star in the early 1934 production *It Happened One Night*, she closed out the year by accepting the lead role of Alice Higgins in Capra's *Broadway Bill*, with a screenplay by Robert Riskin from a Mark Hellinger story. This comedy is another Columbia Capra special about the upper classes driven to lunacy by their riches. Dan Brooks (Warner Baxter) marries money and madness and finally abandons the whole shebang for horse racing. His stallion is Broadway Bill, and Myrna Loy's Alice assists as trainer for the Kentucky Derby.

*EVELYN PRENTICE (1934). With Cora Sue Collins and William Powell*

Unfortunately, *Broadway Bill*, like so many early Capra movies, is practically unavailable. Mocking the rich is as good a hobby in the seventies as it was in 1934, so audiences undoubtedly would enjoy the Capra caper just as they did forty-three years ago. Moreover, they would have the treat of seeing Myrna Loy in one of her warmest roles. Otis Ferguson wrote in 1934, "I have never seen her so fresh and touching and really lovable; but the hand here is her own, one feels, sensitive and firm. Mr. Capra has the wisdom of being able to mold or leave alone, as the case requires."

After *Broadway Bill*, Loy took an extended vacation, staying clear of Metro. She visited Europe and New York—she'd never been to either place before—and returned to Hollywood on the condition that her MGM contract would be improved. She felt overworked and underpaid—the typical complaints of the contract player. Some stars left their studios "on strike" and were never heard from again. Loy left, and when the public clamored for her movies, Louis B. Mayer gave in to her demands.

On loan to Paramount, Loy barnstormed through *Wings in the Dark* (1935) as a stunt flier who saves Cary Grant from self-destruction. This was her first film with Grant, and it wasn't much of an adventure. Their obvious comic talents were drowned by director James Flood, who pushed them instead into heavy suds. Pilot Grant is blinded in a freak accident and helped toward renewed vision, both spiritual and physical, by aviatrix Loy.

Loy does everything for this man. She buys him a seeing-eye dog, which he first wants to kick out of the house, but he can't find the door! Then she hands him her weekly air-circus salary checks, pretending they are from magazine publishers. (Actually his free-lance aeronautics articles have all been rejected.) She is bribing Grant to survive, spoon-feeding him courage so that he can continue his experiments on "blind flying."

The jig seems up when the bank confiscates his plane. However, everything turns out happily: he saves her life, guiding her down through a pea-soup fog by his blind flight methods, and she saves him from suicide—he planned to fly off into the Great Infinity. A flash of reporters' bulbs magically,

*BROADWAY BILL (1934). With Warner Baxter*

*WINGS IN THE DARK (1935). With Cary Grant*

yet somehow expectedly, restores Grant's sight at the film's conclusion.

Anxious to get Loy's name circulating in cinema circles again, MGM produced *Whipsaw* (1935), a cops-and-robbers romance with Loy as a member of a burglar's band. As Vivian Palmer, Loy steals "jools" as well as men's hearts. The chief heart under surveillance belongs to G-Man Spencer Tracy as Ross McBride. Audiences liked the movie, although they could sense (and rightly) that Metro had bought the property with the idea of Powell and Loy and had substituted Tracy only when William Powell became unavailable.

In *Wife Vs. Secretary* (1936), Myrna Loy, as Linda Stanhope, sits anxiously by the telephone for hours each day. She awaits her husband's call, not realizing that Van (Clark Gable) is putting over a big business deal and not putting the make on his loyal and capable secretary, Whitey Wilson (Jean Harlow). Besides, Whitey has a beau of her own, played by lanky Jimmy Stewart in his fourth screen appearance.

The jealous worm rots the core of Stanhope's golden three-year marriage. Loy weeps through *Wife Vs. Secretary*, sniffling sometimes from the nasty cold she catches at the ice rink but mostly because she's desperately unhappy, feeling witless and worthless. This wife has

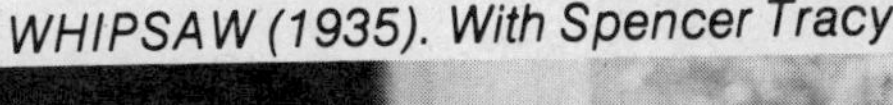

*WHIPSAW (1935). With Spencer Tracy*

WIFE VS. SECRETARY (1936).
With Clark Gable

so much spare time that she fantasizes the most elaborate romantic scheming, with lewd thoughts of the foxy blonde secretary making brilliant use of her husband's office hours.

The title of Clarence Brown's film suggests the prime male fantasy—two women slugging it out for the irresistible man, who needs to do nothing but be his clever self. Yet the truly great Loy scenes are friendly moments with Harlow, who is a strange bird for the "other woman," not a sluttish bombshell but utterly tender with the saddened Linda. When Loy is about to run away to Europe, Harlow stops her at the boat and convinces wife to return to husband.

In retrospect, some of the subtle appeal of Clarence Brown's film comes from the complete reversal of the expected stereotypes in the roles of the two women. As Loy explained it, "The sexiest wife I ever did was in *Wife Vs. Secretary*. That woman had one foot in bed through the whole story, while Jean Harlow, who was supposedly the other woman, was very proper throughout."

Loy returned to perfect wifedom and William Powell in *The Great Ziegfeld* (1936)—their first film together since *Evelyn Prentice* in 1934. Loy bleached her hair a light reddish gold and became Billie Burke for her part—the Great Ziegfeld's second wife. Her role was small but vastly important, coming in toward the film's conclusion to soften the blow of the master showman's sudden separation from Anna Held (Luise Rainer), the first Mrs. Ziegfeld.

Ziegfeld and Burke meet at a party, when Loy enters the film by practically waltzing down the staircase, looking more like a Follies' showgirl than a star of the legitimate theater. Soon they are chatting on the terrace, and shortly after, the two are married. They push ahead, and the quiet, sympathetic, perfect wife gives birth to Flo's child, lends him money, and supplies emotional support. When Flo comes home depressed after the flop of his Broadway productions, Billie coos, "Flo, I'm disappointed in you. I didn't think you'd ever lose confidence in yourself." With those stirring words in mind, Ziegfeld goes out and creates four Broadway spectaculars: *Rio Rita, Rosalie, The Three Musketeers*, and *Show Boat*.

*The Great Ziegfeld* was not a great example of biographical cinema. The musical numbers are stolen from Busby Berkeley, and the movie goes on for many screen hours, without quality ever equaling quantity. Reviewers criticized Loy's Burke. But really what could be expected with the real life Billie Burke residing just across town?

At last in 1936, Myrna Loy took her first real-life nuptial vows.

America's perfect wife had found her ostensibly perfect mate, movie producer Arthur Hornblow, Jr., on the *Arrowsmith* set five years earlier, and now they were betrothed in Mexico. Without much of a honeymoon, Loy popped back to work at Metro.

Even Loy's most faithful fans could not exonerate *Petticoat Fever* (1936), which *New York Times* reviewer Frank Nugent diagnosed as "suffering from a severe attack of whimsy." When a plane falls from the sky, Irene Campion (Loy) is deposited in Labrador on Dascom Dinsmore's doorstep. Robert Montgomery plays Dinsmore, a churl who hasn't seen a "petticoat" in the two years he's been residing in the north country, so naturally he goes bananas about Loy. She forsakes her knightly lover, Sir James Felton (Reginald Owen), for her rich but loony pursuer. They remain together for some warm connubial nights in the cold arctic clime. But audiences who saw *Petticoat Fever* never warmed up.

After *Ziegfeld*, Loy was reunited with Warner Baxter (the *Broadway Bill* team, sans thoroughbred) in *To Mary—With Love* (1936). The movie centered on the ups and downs of Mary's

*THE GREAT ZIEGFELD (1936). With William Powell*

*With Arthur Hornblow, Jr. following their marriage in 1936*

*On the set of PETTICOAT FEVER (1936) with director George Fitzmaurice*

marriage, 1925-35, to Jock Wallace, which conveniently coincided with key historical happenings in that decade. They wed at the Waldorf while political bosses celebrate the Jimmy Walker victory. They quarrel while Charles Lindbergh is honored with a midtown ticker-tape parade. After a couple of confusing love affairs (he with Claire Trevor, she with Ian Hunter), they resurrect their crumbling marriage in time to enjoy the New Deal.

The reviews were poor, but Loy managed to pull off one stunning scene. Learning of her baby's death in a hospital, Loy turns from Baxter and mutters with tragic irony, "They say the movies should be more like life; I think life should be more like the movies." Loy's commentary: "I played this scene away from him: to have reacted directly to what he said would have been too emphatic and have turned the moment to bathos."

Enough tears for Loy and time for comedy: the mirthful *Libeled Lady* (1936) with the hefty cast of Myrna Loy, William Powell, Jean Harlow and Spencer Tracy.

A tabloid headline screams across the screen: "Peer's Wife Routs Rich Playgirl!" The face smeared across the front page be-

*TO MARY—WITH LOVE (1936). With Warner Baxter*

*LIBELED LADY (1936). With William Powell*

longs to Connie Allenbury (Myrna Loy). "Stop the presses!" frantic reporters shout—the newsroom commotion stems from the fact that "the Allenbury girl" was nowhere near the peer nor his wife when the scandal broke, and the rich playgirl intends to sue the paper for five million dollars. That leaves a fat hole in the pocketbook of editor Warren Haggerty (Spencer Tracy). So he cancels his wedding to Gladys Benton (Jean Harlow)—obviously for the zillionth time, which annoys her terribly—and pays off his Lothario ex-employee Bill Chandler (William Powell) to marry his Gladys and then seduce Connie Allenbury. That way, Gladys can sue for alienation of affection, thereby making good the libelous story. The expected happens: Connie and Bill fall in love; Gladys also wants to stay with Bill, and Warren wants to punch Bill in the nose. Everything gets mixed up—but by the end, Bill catches Connie's admiration, Gladys gets her man, and Warren is saved from the bankruptcy of the libel suit.

For a modest Montana woman,

Myrna Loy in the mid-thirties

Loy fit the haughty rich girl mold very nicely. With her nose pushed in the air and a mink draped across her lithe shoulders, Loy's Connie snubs Bill, reporters, and nouveau riche society hunters with aristocratic disdain. When Bill trails Loy and her father (Walter Connolly) onto an ocean liner, trying to make contact for his planned seduction, she is too smart to see the man with anything but keen suspicion. She looks skeptical when Bill (after cramming on angling manuals all night) talks trout to her wealthy papa, a fishing aficionado.

Finally, Allenbury invites him trout fishing. Following days of desperate tutorials, Bill discovers his tennis backhand useful in casting and joins the Allenbury clan in the swift waters of upstate New York. Connie smirks as he slips downstream—out of sight of his host. A current tucks him under, tumbles his manual away, and leaves him helpless to catch a fish. But magically, the big "Wall Eyes," Allenbury's underwater nemesis—top of the "Most Wanted" trout list—practically leaps into Bill's arms. In short time, Connie does likewise.

They swim to an abandoned boat house for quick romance before the screwball comedy turns predictably nasty when Gladys and Warren arrive with camera and flash bulbs, ready to turn the libel story into hot news headlines.

*Libeled Lady* is among the greatest comedies of the thirties, made by Metro-Goldwyn-Mayer's most underrated comedy director, Jack Conway, and helped along by the masterful rapport of the leads. Off screen, Loy and Harlow were dear friends, partly because Loy and Powell were such pals and Harlow and Powell were lovers. A John Pascal 1964 biography of Harlow could still infuriate Loy. "That book about her life was a pack of lies," the actress bristled in a *New York Times* interview. She described her platinum blonde friend to David Chierichetti as " . . . a quiet, dignified woman who seldom even went out," although "she could tell you off . . . when she got mad." A tribute to Loy must include praise also for Harlow.

In Myrna Loy's busy year of 1936, *The Thin Man* team got together for a second crack at murder in *After the Thin Man.* Barely back home in San Francisco from New York and the Wynant caper, Nick and Nora find strange people partying in their living room, an empty refrigerator in their kitchen, and soon a dead man on Nora's relatives' front lawn.

The body belongs to one of Nora's worthless in-laws, a black sheep who left his sweet wife to run wild with a nightclub singer. Nick and Nora might have left the case for the dogs—Asta and Co.—but the police accuse Nora's cousin Selma (Elissa Landi). With her love for danger, Nora coaxes indolent Nick into taking the case and taking her along on the hunt. As in the original *Thin Man*, the Charles's method of detection relies more on swilling whiskey than scouting suspects. They stay up all night scrambling eggs and chasing Asta who swallowed a clue attached to a rock thrown through their kitchen window; then they sleep all day, finally eating those eggs at six P.M. and wondering why the "breakfast" paper is the late edition.

Again Nora is the butt of trickster Nick's prime jokes, including having Nora tossed into the "fish tank" by the local cops. Who done it? If it matters at all—and in *Thin Man* movies, it matters little—the skinny, sweet-faced David (Jimmy Stewart), Selma's rejected and resentful boy friend from years ago, proves to be the culprit.

The one problem in the film is that wirehaired pup Asta, who digs holes, steals secrets, and generally is visible too much of the time. As for the future of the *Thin Man* series, Nora sits knitting baby booties, smooches the undaunted Nick, and declares, "And you call yourself a detective?" Did W. S. Van Dyke guess there was box office in babies?

In 1937 critics agreed that John Stahl's *Parnell* was banal pap. Metro cut the grit from the life of Irish revolutionary and Home-Rule advocate Charles Stewart Parnell's life and called it "biography." The skeleton of facts remain, but the dynamics and the historical context are missing. As every student of Irish history knows, Captain Willie O'Shea chose a very trying time to divorce his wife Kate, naming Parnell in the adultery case: it was the moment of deciding Irish Home Rule. But the political insinuations of the deed were as unimportant for MGM as the issue of Irish independence. What counted was the potential romantic value of the O'Shea-Parnell scandal. MGM figured that the notorious affair, enacted by Myrna Loy and Clark Gable, Hollywood's King and

*AFTER THE THIN MAN (1936). With William Powell and Sam Levene*

*PARNELL (1937). With (left to right) Montagu Love, Clark Gable, Edna May Oliver, Billie Burke, and Alan Marshal*

Queen, could spice up the studio's box office receipts. Little did they know.

*Parnell* was the only pre-World War II Gable picture to lose money, a veritable potato famine for MGM. His super-heroic Parnell, emerging like Christ to help the Irish peasants, didn't go over too well with moviegoers. As for Loy, she looked grand as she ennobled the women's section of Parliament, the bleachers, where she sat worshipfully through Parnell's finest speeches. (Director Stahl always framed her lovingly through sections of grating, separating her from the riffraff with whom she sat). But her character remains blurred.

Loy's Kate gyrates somewhere between a scandal-defying rebel and a silly sorority girl. She travels to Parnell's rooms in the middle of the night and brings him back to her home, magnificently defying all codes of decency—then she runs to her Aunt Bea for permission, like an adolescent with an embarrassingly dirty joke to tell. Feeling uncomfortable in the role, Loy worked much too hard at being effective and ended ineffective. In Frank Nugent's words in *The New York Times*, "Miss Loy is about as fiery as a Wellesley daisy chain."

"Bring on the clowns!" MGM bosses hollered in desperation after *Parnell*'s strained seriousness. To dispel *Parnell*'s pernicious effects on Loy's screen popularity, Metro magnates promptly dusted off her proper mate, William Powell, and cast the pair as a zany iconoclast and a stuffed-shirt clothes designer, Powell and Loy respectively, in *Double Wedding* (1937).

The screwball shenanigans concern a batty bohemian, Charlie Lodge—painter, playwright and streetcorner philosopher—and Margit Agnew—a well-organized, well-heeled monster of a fashion designer. Margit controls the placement of mannequins in her shop and dominates her sister's life at home, telling her sibling not only what to eat for breakfast but at what temperature to set her bath water. The overbearing Margit finally pushes one step too far in arranging her sister's wedding, as she both sets the date and chooses the mate! While Irene (Florence Rice) is perfectly happy to marry Waldo Beaver (John Beal), she's sick of her sister's meddling and of Waldo's passivity and cowardice. To rebel, Irene breaks the engagement and announces she's running off with Charlie. Enter William Powell.

Charlie is everything wrong and contrary to Margit. He lives in a throw her money away! He walks he's still friends with the wife he divorced because she wouldn't throw her money away. He walks around in a raccoon coat and falls in love with Loy for no other reason except that she is so hostile. After much hectic slapstick activity, Margit finally confesses that she, in turn, loves the crazy artist.

The comedy of *Double Wedding* is strained. Loy rarely smiles as she faces off in this love war with Powell. They battle beyond the call of duty in an uncommonly unfunny way. Somewhere either in Ferenc Molnar's original play or Richard Thorpe's screen transformation, the fun gets kicked out of the romance and turns the comedy into a long, humorless lecture on the need for humor and spontaneity.

Not long after *Double Wedding*, Loy was back out in the cold, jilted by Walter Pidgeon for the moneyed Rosalind Russell in MGM's *Man-Proof* (1938). However, Pidgeon returns from his honeymoon with a renewed eye for his estranged ex-girlfriend, who now has found solace in the loving arms of faithful Franchot Tone. What should Myrna Loy do? Her pressure and indecision lead Loy to "put on one of the gracefulest upper-class drunks of recent record," said B. R. Crisler admiringly in a generally indifferent *New York Times* review of this trifling love story.

Loy wanted to prove that she could play drama as effectively as comedy. The proper part came

*DOUBLE WEDDING (1937). With William Powell and Jessie Ralph*

*MAN-PROOF (1938). With Rosalind Russell*

from Victor Fleming, who cast her as Ann Barton in *Test Pilot* (1938). Testing the mechanics of matrimony and aviation along with Loy are Clark Gable as pilot Jim Lane and Spencer Tracy as the gum-cracking Gunner Sloane. The heavy-duty trio, playing at the top of their form in a mighty Spig Wead screenplay, led Frank S. Nugent to exclaim in *The New York Times*, "Leo, the trademark lion, can stop yawning now and roar with some of his old enthusiasm."

The story of *Test Pilot* is the familiar aviation-and-romance mixture. Like *The Wizard of Oz*'s swirling tornado, Jim Lane crash-lands in Ann Barton's Kansas cornfield. When Jim takes off again, Ann is with him in the cockpit. They are on their way to a preacher and also to the land of flying circuses. Ann is sharp and college educated, but she is a country girl still, Montana Myrna lost among the grizzled veteran test pilots. These good old boys greet death with gin and sober up only long enough to fly the next run or twirl around a pylon.

*TEST PILOT (1938). With Clark Gable*

*TOO HOT TO HANDLE (1938). With Clark Gable*

Ann shares Jim with Gunner—the third foot of this familiar triangle. For luck, Gunner slaps a wad of gum on Jim's plane and blows a farewell kiss in the direction of his taxiing ship. Afterward, Ann and Gunner stand together on the ground, chewing gum and fingernails in anticipation of their beloved's return to earth. In such circumstances, a woman can either leave her man or drink with him. Loy's Ann does a lot of drinking before leaving her man, following the death of Gunner in an air crash.

Ann and Jim reconcile and he quits flying to teach. Now he chews gum and sticks it on his students' planes. Ann meets him at the field. They are parents now with a child in arms. Jim looks longingly at the planes taking off and mutters, "A man spends his whole life trying to get somewhere, but he gets nowhere, back where he started." Meanwhile, Ann smiles brightly. She has won her man to safe domesticity—and besides, Ann Barton is Myrna Loy's favorite role of her entire film career. She has stated she likes *Test Pilot* even better than the *Thin Man* series. But for Gable's Jim Lane, everything is lost. The domesticated man is the emasculated man. The closing image is Gable looking upward toward his fliers and away from Loy—in the broader scope, she's lost, too.

Loy took to the air while Gable remained earthbound for their next production together, Jack Conway's *Too Hot to Handle* (1938). The film opens at an unbelievably high pitch, with Gable and Walter Pidgeon as competing newsreel photographers on assignment to capture the Shanghai War on celluloid. They do anything for a story: create bogus bombing raids, photograph fake orphans, and use toy planes and firecrackers to simulate a war for the homefront audience. Eventually, too, they involve Loy, as Alma, the crack aviatrix, in their devious plots. But the minute Loy enters the frame, her plane colliding with Gable's camera van, the wonderfully cynical comedy, every bit as seamy and nasty as a Hecht-MacArthur concoction, grinds to a dreary stop. Loy's part is simply terrible, astoundingly humorless.

*Too Hot to Handle* moves back to the States and wastes time and energy on unravelling the reporters' chicanery, but the movie picks up ever so slightly for a last reel hunt through the Amazon for Loy's missing brother. In an outrageously racist scene, Gable enters a village of black voodoo tribesmen to rescue the kidnapped lad, then projects newsreel footage onto a rock to prove that he is also a Big Medicine Man. *King Kong* revisited. And so it goes—the buffoonery is uninspired and insipid, never recovering the magnificent momentum and wit of *Too Hot to Handle*'s first glorious half hour.

Loy, grounded for most of *Too Hot to Handle*, walked next into *Lucky Night* (1939), an adolescent farce with a silly script. She plays the daughter of a steel magnate who marries an unemployed paint salesman (Robert Taylor). He thinks he's a wild iconoclast, but most of the "humor" centers on their struggles at happy homemaking. *Lucky Night* wasn't such a lucky break for Loy. The *New York Times* complained that it possessed "one of the most embarrassingly bad scripts ever to be taken seriously by a producer, a director and a cast."

MGM loaned their perfect wife to Twentieth Century-Fox for *The Rains Came* (1939), from the best-selling Louis Bromfield novel. Fox wanted Loy and Loy wanted "her director," MGM's Clarence Brown, and she got him for the picture. But Loy didn't always enjoy Fox's interfering producer, Darryl F. Zanuck who "still saw me as a vamp even after all the perfect wife publicity." Loy told David Chierichetti, "I don't know how many times he called me on the carpet to tell me I wasn't playing the role right, but I stuck to my guns."

The problem might have been

*LUCKY NIGHT (1939). With Robert Taylor*

*THE RAINS CAME (1939). As Lady Edwina Esketh*

*ANOTHER THIN MAN (1939). With William Powell*

that Brown tried transforming Loy's Lady Edwina Esketh into Greta Garbo, a vamp changed half way through into an angel. As Frank Nugent mused, "Myrna Loy's Lady Esketh represents the hapless struggle of an actress who can't help being 'sympathetic' with a role that requires her . . . to be a shameless hussy."

Bored and restless, Edwina marries money—a dull and pompous man (Nigel Bruce) who lists the names of her paramours in a secret black book. Among the string of males, he includes Tom Ransome (George Brent), Edwina's former lover whom she tries seducing once again in a darkened corner of the Maharani's palace. While lightning slithers across the room, announcing the coming squall, Edwina's cigarette smoke leaps and glistens across her face like one of Concha's veils in Dietrich's *The Devil is a Woman*. Ultimately, however, her love for the kindly Indian surgeon Rama Safti (Tyrone Power) transforms her evil into virtue.

As the title says, the rains come, followed by quakes, floods, and malaria. Edwina (with her husband safely dead) stays in Ranchipur, joining Doctor Safti at work in the hospital, nursing patients and washing floors. A good girl again, Edwina still must pay for her sins by dying. Consumed by disease, she slips from life, whispering to Rama, "You are India." With her titian hair spread across the pillow, she looks truly like a fallen angel. The combined talents of Loy and Brown saved *The Rains Came* from woeful melodrama, but it was still time for *Another Thin Man* (1939).

The third in the series, the movie brings a Bonnie Prince Charles into the kooky family—a boy named Nicky, Junior, who replaces Asta for the cutesy jokes award. It's at Junior's first birthday party that Nick, Senior, gathers together all suspects for the traditional dénouement. But infant Nicky functions most significantly as his parents' domesticator. They start calling each other "Mummy and Daddy" and start worrying as much about baby formula as they do about the hidden key to the liquor cabinet.

*Another Thin Man* did very well, even with the novel addition of Nicky Junior and the coy family humor thrown into the plot. In this one instance, Dashiell Hammett himself wrote the screenplay. After the recent movie duds for Myrna Loy, *Another Thin Man* lifted everybody's spirits. MGM was loving Loy again, and her public adored her. But before her next film with William Powell, called *I Love You Again*, Loy took a brief vacation from Hollywood. In real life, the perfect wife was experiencing marital difficulties.

Myrna Loy took a break from acting in an attempt to repair the faltering alliance with Arthur Hornblow. She visited her childhood home in Montana before returning to Metro. There the triumphant triumvirate—Woody Van Dyke, Powell and Loy—went to work on another screwball comedy, *I Love You Again* (1940). Ironically, this farce centered on a marriage already at the divorce courts, saved by a blow on the head.

Larry Wilson (Powell), a stuffed shirt, is struck on the noggin while rescuing an inebriated shipmate, Doc Ryan (Frank McHugh) from an overboard spill. When Wilson regains his senses, he awakens from the amnesia which has affected him for the last nine years. He's not really Wilson at all, he remembers, but George Carey, a con man. And yet this Wilson appears to be rich, so Carey decides to continue as Wilson for a while and abscond with his money. Once home, however, Carey meets Wilson's wife, Kay (Loy). Instantly smitten, he decides to stay on forever.

The problem: Kay hates her husband Wilson; he is married to the Rotary Club and Lions Club, not to her. When Wilson coos, "You've turned my head," she snaps back, "I've often wished I could turn your head—on a spit over a low fire."

## SCREWBALL LADY

He flirts with Kay, telling fanciful stories of love birds' mating rituals. She responds by dumping a bowl of eggs on his head. He takes her on a shopping spree, buying nearly non-existent negligees—black lace, backless, and expensive, too. By now Kay's guessing—this devilish dandy can't be her skinflint Larry.

In the end, Kay learns the truth about George Carey, including his new plot to cheat the community. She forgives him. He reforms, and the film is about to end happily ever after, until a gangster hits George over the head. Will he get amnesia again? Kay sneaks up behind to smash him again, but George pops up and kisses her and they're in love again. Powell gets the best jokes, yet Loy also has some wacky moments. *I Love You Again* is a fun-filled, expert comedy, with credit certainly due to director Woody Van Dyke, at home and having a jolly, boisterous time with his *Thin Man* team.

Myrna Loy sports a gold wedding band in Robert Z. Leonard's *Third Finger, Left Hand* (1940), but she is not married to anybody. She wears the ring for self-preservation from the boss's green-eyed wife and the wide-eyed wolves who come barking at her door. The trouble begins when she really falls in love with Melvyn Douglas, for

*I LOVE YOU AGAIN (1940). With Frank McHugh and William Powell*

she refuses to give up the ghost of her non-existent husband.

The story is strained, as MGM temporarily overdosed on Myrna Loy screwball comedies. Critic Otis Ferguson, who had enjoyed *Libeled Lady* and *The Thin Man*, was so unimpressed that he actually forgot to review *Third Finger, Left Hand* in his regular *New Republic* column. Slipping in a short review the ensuing week, Ferguson complained that "this type of MGM spoof and glitter story of love fighting itself off through curious complications and then fighting itself right back again" had simply grown wearying.

Jack Conway's *Love Crazy* (1941) is a loonybin comedy, somewhere between Howard Hawks's later *Monkey Business* and a Daffy Duck cartoon. Susan and Steve (Loy and Powell) start celebrating their third anniversary by necking in their darkened bedroom, and who knows where they would have ended if Susan's mother (Florence Bates) hadn't rung the doorbell. The old gorgon not only stays for dinner but trips on a rug, sending Susan on an errand and leaving Steve alone and annoyed on their anniversary.

Soon Susan and Steve are a mess because he has a drink with a buxom ex-girlfriend (Gail Patrick) he's met in the elevator. Seeking revenge for his hanky panky, Susan becomes entangled with the neighboring archery champ, brawny and brainless Ward Willoughby (Jack Carson). It seems like the divorce courts are next on the agenda, but Steve feigns insanity to wiggle out of it. Predictably, Susan commits him willingly!

For the audience, the real fun begins when Steve flees from the mental institution and visits Susan at home. To escape detection, he disguises himself as his own sister, donning a powdered wig, knitting breasts of yarn, and even shaving clean the immortal William Powell mustache!

Miraculously, Steve averts catastrophe. The cops confuse Willoughby for Steve, and cart off Robin Hood. Susan learns the truth about her long past anniversary incident and decides to share the bedroom with "Steve's sister." Her nagging mother yells, "Get a good night's sleep," just as Steve opens the door. He is still in drag. Are the screen's most sophisticated couple about to embark on a Hollywood first—a transsexual love affair?

*Shadow of the Thin Man* was released in November 1941, only a

*THIRD FINGER, LEFT HAND (1940). With Melvyn Douglas*

few short weeks before the bombing of Pearl Harbor. (America's participation in the war is prefigured by the appearance of Nick Junior in sailor's uniform.) With this fourth film of the series and the further softening of Nick and Nora Charles, Frank Nugent's cautionary warning was borne out: "The law of diminishing returns tends to put any comedy on a reducing diet, and maybe a thin man thinned to the point of emaciation."

The mystery opens with a new pecking order: Nick holding a leash at the end of which toddles Nick Junior, who also holds a leash behind which trails Asta. Nora is Mama, separate from the male family members. She gets the boys home by shaking a pitcher of martinis, but when it comes to dinner, Nora insists—at Junior's request—that Nick drink milk. The domestication of the Charleses continues. Nick's gun hasn't been loaded since Junior started teething.

While the film has some great moments—Nick and Nora at the wrestling match, Nora yelling good wishes to the athlete who pauses in the ring to thank her—it's mostly overdone. The jokes are louder and sillier, and the murder mystery it-

*LOVE CRAZY (1941). With William Powell and Florence Bates*

*SHADOW OF THE THIN MAN (1941). With William Powell*

*THE THIN MAN GOES HOME (1944). With Asta and William Powell*

self is confusing and quite boring. Especially after the outrageous daffiness of *I Love You Again* and the terrific good humor of *Love Crazy, Shadow of the Thin Man* was disappointing, less than a shadow of the original.

Two weeks after Metro's release of *Shadow of the Thin Man*, bombs fell on Pearl Harbor. The world awakened to Roosevelt's war announcement. Anti-fascist Myrna Loy demonstrated why her name graced the top of Adolf Hitler's hate sheet. (She got there years earlier when she was among the first to condemn the invasion of Czechoslovakia and to denounce the Munich pact.) Now she dropped out of Hollywood to join the war effort. She did not make another film for three years.

During this period of artistic inactivity, she spoiled her "perfect wife" title by obtaining a Mexican divorce from hubby Hornblow and marrying rent-a-car entrepreneur John D. Hertz, Jr., six days later. On June 6, 1942, Loy moved to New York where she spent the next two years with the Red Cross, entertaining wounded soldiers,

*THE THIN MAN GOES HOME (1944). With William Powell, Lucile Watson, and Harry Davenport*

visiting hospitals and generally boosting morale. In 1944, Loy made a second divorce trip to Mexico. Then Myrna Loy went home again to Hollywood, MGM, and her old stand-by, Nick Charles, to film *The Thin Man Goes Home* (1944).

Nick, Jr. is growing up now and in school and so thankfully out of the picture. Nick and Nora are on their way home to visit Nick's parents and it's much more fun watching these suave adults behave as children than watching them relate to their own child. For the trip to see his proper progenitors, Nick is on the wagon, drinking apple cider out of his whiskey flask. And Nora, concerned about the Oedipal anguishes between the Charles men, wants Nick to do something special, solve any old case, while at his childhood home. Perhaps that way his father will respect his silly son at last.

There are many bright moments in this *Thin Man* movie, such as Nora's late night prowl through the center of town as she follows

*With best man Admiral "Bull" Halsey and groom Gene Markey at her wedding on January 3, 1946*

the man she thinks is the murderer. Actually he is Nick's secret partner, Brogan (Edward Brophy), on assignment to lead Nora on a wild goose chase and teach her a lesson. He takes her past the bus terminal, a barbershop, into a pool hall, and practically into the Men's Room. Nora hangs on.

The problem in all the later *Thin Man* movies is that Nora becomes somewhat of a dolt. She abandons her upper class, modish, Katharine Hepburn comic style and becomes Lucille Ball or Gracie Allen. Lucy and Gracie are fun, but we expect intelligence and wisdom from Nora.

After *The Thin Man Goes Home*, Loy ended her contract with Metro. Although she promised availability for another *Thin Man* picture or any other Powell coupling, Loy was free to pursue her other interest: politics.

In 1945, Myrna Loy attended the San Francisco conference at which the United Nations was created. She later served as a United States representative to UNESCO. She was the first Hollywood personality to accept such a position, and, in 1949, Mike Mansfield, then in the House of Representatives, spoke in Congress, praising the work of this other Montanan.

On January 3, 1946, Loy married for a third time. Her new husband was Gene Markey, Hollywood writer and producer, formerly wedded to Joan Bennett and Hedy Lamarr. Admiral "Bull" Halsey acted as best man and Colonel John Ford gave the bride away in a ceremony at the Naval Chapel in Terminal Island, San Pedro.

After the wedding, Loy returned to the screen, this time as Don Ameche's wife in *So Goes My Love* (1946). Ameche, the screen's eternal Alexander Graham Bell, plays another quirky nineteenth century inventor, Hiram Stephen Maxim, responsible for such items as the curling iron and the Maxim gun. Loy has eccentric ideas of her own but they are about Love. She travels from Boston to New York to Brooklyn to catch her man. The Universal film is the very defini-

*SO GOES MY LOVE (1946). With Don Ameche*

ion of "mildly amusing." As the *New York Times* said, much more colorfully, "It is the type of entertainment which most likely will sit well with those who can devour a double peach melba and come up smiling."

Not so her next picture, the indisputable Hollywood classic, *The Best Years of Our Lives*.

# THE BEST—AND WORST—YEARS OF HER LIFE

In 1946, Myrna Loy earned top billing in the year's top picture, William Wyler's *The Best Years of Our Lives*. She also won the Brussels Film Festival Award for her performance as Milly Stephenson, the sergeant's wife.

*The Best Years of Our Lives* relates the return home of three World War II veterans, who timidly face civilian readjustment. The home front isn't the same as when they left, nor are they. Homer Parrish (non-actor Harold Russell) lost his hands in combat and fears his mother's tears at the sight of his hooks. Air Force Captain Fred Derry (Dana Andrews) is just a soda jerk at home and from the wrong side of the tracks. Sergeant Al Stephenson (Fredric March) returns from fighting to his confining banker's chair, his bourgeois apartment, his now grown-up children, and a wife, Milly, whom he hasn't seen in years.

Al worries, "The thing I'm most scared of is everybody's going to want to rehabilitate me." But Milly takes readjustment at a snail's pace. Milly is reticent, reserved, the silent type who conveys her deepest emotions through almost imperceptible body movements. William Wyler's masterly scene: when Al comes home, he knocks at the door but doesn't let the children speak a greeting and spoil the surprise. A voice, Loy's voice, calls from somewhere outside the frame, "Who's at the door?" There's a pause and the camera cuts to Milly bending over to set the table. She repeats, "Who's at the door?" And when no one answers again, she twitches her shoulders in subtle understanding, stoops to put her dishes on the table, finishing her task at hand, and enters the hall where Al still stands. He embraces her for a long, quiet time. He holds her the way anyone would want to be held by a lover.

The children look on smiling. Gregg Toland's camera cuts away to the children and then back to Milly and Al, and still they hold each other. "I look terrible," she grumbles. "It's not fair of you to bust in on us like this." She asks, "Are you all right?" and they embrace again. Then Milly makes a phone call to break a dinner engagement with people she's met during the war. She nods her head vigorously with a huge grin on her face, repeating at intervals, "Yes . . . yes . . . yes." That "yes" speaks volumes—she's so happy he's home. The scene is extremely touching, as memorable as the return from the war to Mae Marsh of the Little Colonel in Griffith's *The Birth of a Nation*, or as the final re-

*THE BEST YEARS OF OUR LIVES (1946). With Fredric March and Teresa Wright*

conciliation in John Ford's *The Searchers*.

Like Nick's Nora, Al's Milly is a totally tolerant woman and sensitive to her spouse's troubles. Al tries with all his strength, relaxing in a chair on his first night home, but he grows restless and promptly decides to rehabilitate himself by taking his wife and daughter Peggy (Teresa Wright) drinking. He gets drunk as he and Milly dance cheek to cheek. She gets him home and puts him to bed, twisting his arm to roll him over as if she's spent a life turning drunks.

If *The Best Years of Our Lives* centers on the men, the story really depends upon the women who nurture them back to emotional health after the war. As mother and lover, Milly represents the very soul of the family and society, the heart that keeps the blood beating through civilization.

*The Best Years of Our Lives* is very homespun and apple pie in some respects. The reaffirmation of good old American values of family and neighborly kindness and love between husband and wife may seem trying to the cynics

*THE BEST YEARS OF OUR LIVES (1946).*
*With Fredric March and Ray Collins*

of post-Viet Nam, post-Watergate America. Yet to many people in late forties America, paranoid, isolationist, and scared of the Iron Curtain, *The Best Years* was considered anti-American and found its way on the special list of "commie propaganda" drawn up by rightists in 1948. "Sam Goldwyn was a very courageous man to make that picture," says Loy. "Everybody warned him against it." The actress recalls the period, and not nostalgically: "You could feel this cold wind blow into Hollywood . . . There was a clash between liberals and conservatives . . . A terror had seized the whole country, and in Hollywood, the terror was that the communists would take over. So the right wing organized. They engaged in a witch hunt."

Loy did not go unscathed. In October 1946, the libeled lady threatened a million-dollar law suit against a Hollywood trade magazine which had accused her of communist affiliations. The branding was attributed to Matthew Woll, who retracted the statement, commenting later that he "found her war record excellent and her Americanism beyond dispute." The magazine was the *Hollywood Reporter*, and the editorial itself

*THE BEST YEARS OF OUR LIVES (1946).*
*With Fredric March and Teresa Wright*

*THE BACHELOR AND THE BOBBY-SOXER (1947). With Cary Grant*

*SONG OF THE THIN MAN (1947). With Keenan Wynn and William Powell*

was written by Publisher/Editor W. R. (Billy) Wilkerson.

After *The Best Years*, the moviegoing public clamored for more Loy. So RKO cast her as the fearsome Judge Margaret Turner, who sentences Cary Grant to "time" dating her lollypop teenaged sister (Shirley Temple) in *The Bachelor and the Bobby-Soxer* (1947). Judge Turner hopes that her silly sibling will be cured of her puppy love crush on Grant, the artist.

The film opens teasingly with Loy asleep in a darkened room, her sexual identity hidden beneath the bed quilts. Later, when she puts on her judge's robe, her psychiatrist uncle moans, "Exit the woman, enter the judge. More's the pity." Much like Loy's 1937 picture, *Double Wedding*, this domineering older sister must be sensitized to her own romantic impulses. But unlike *Double Wedding*, Loy's judge Turner isn't stern and unsmiling. A firm hand seems to be a good idea for sassy Shirley Temple—not just within the film but off camera as well. According to Loy, Temple was " . . . full of tricks. When she knew the photo raphers were coming to take pictures of me, she sneaked old flashbulbs into their cameras."

Typical of too many of her comedies, Loy stands around as the "straight man." Meanwhile Grant gets laughs attending high school basketball with Shirley Temple and participating in marathon races to gain Loy's approval and attention. Gradually Margaret and Richard fall in love, and little sister has a Temple tantrum over their romance. The oldsters get together anyway, flying off to Chicago without Loy having to sacrifice her career. Good judgment for Cary Grant.

The call was for another *Thin Man* story. In 1947, *Song of the Thin Man* was released. Here the ancient night life routine gets the super sleuths involved with crime again. While they are aboard a gambling yacht, the bandleader gets plugged from behind. The music stops and Nick and Nora Charles are at work. They drag around to all-night jazz joints, and much of the film's humor derives from the square Charles's encounters with hip musicians. The be-bop and jive talk runs right past them.

In this *Thin Man* exercise, Loy finally gets a real chance at detec-

*MR. BLANDINGS BUILDS HIS DREAM HOUSE (1948). With Cary Grant*

*THE RED PONY (1949). With Shepperd Strudwick*

tion, visiting a nearly catatonic witness in a mental institution. She tries to pull information from his half-wasted brain, until he hysterically starts waving a gun in her face.

Domesticated or not, *Song of the Thin Man* proved, at least for the *New York Times* critic, that, "Nick and Nora are as good company as they ever were . . ." But even good company must part sometime, and *Song of the Thin Man* was an elegiac song of farewell. Thirteen years after their screen marriage, Nick and Nora parted cordially in this last of the series. With Myrna Loy's walk-on tribute to her dear friend Bill Powell in *The Senator Was Indiscreet* (1947), Hollywood's favorite, happiest and most perfect couple split up for good.

In 1948 Loy teamed a third time with Cary Grant as Muriel Blandings in *Mr. Blandings Builds His Dream House*. Based on the popular Eric Hodgins novel, the movie is a fanciful tale about a family of four, going crazy in their claustrophobic Manhattan apartment. They seek the natural life in Connecticut, purchasing a ramshackle mansion no sturdier than a bird's nest in winter.

The refurbishing begins with the help of a visionary architect. Muriel battles for bathrooms and closets, a greenhouse, pantry, flowered wallpaper and fireplace. Cary Grant's Jim Blandings cries and kicks his heels when he sees bills zooming into the thousand-dollar range. There's nothing for the man to do but work harder at his advertising job and sell more "Wham Hams."

*Mr. Blandings* was a perfect extension for Loy's perfect wife image. Her comic touch did not diminish even with the demise of the *Thin Man* series. While Cary Grant clowns more outrageously, Loy still shares the antics of primitive suburban living. The couple freeze together through the night in their fifteen-thousand-dollar squiredom which lacks windows, heat, electricity and floor boards, and they get stuck together in the little supply room after the workers leave for the weekend.

As an answer to the post-World-War II housing shortage, the picture may be a flop. But for chuckles, *Mr. Blandings* is an unqualified success. As the *Times* critic wrote, "The business . . . of a man putting a roof over his family's head is so . . . entertaining and so conducive to a feeling of goodwill that, made the experience of a nation, it could change the destiny of the world."

Lewis Milestone, who directed the film classic, *Of Mice and Men* (1939), later brought to the screen a second Steinbeck short novel, *The Red Pony* (1949), scripted by the author himself. "Milestone has done an advantageous thing in shooting much of the picture on an actual California ranch," wrote *New York Times* critic Bosley Crowther, "And the one real dramatic crisis—the red pony's agonizing death—has been pictured by him with fidelity to the stabbing shock of Mr. Steinbeck's tale." Myrna Loy returned at last to her own rural background in playing the boy's rancher mother. Interestingly she seems a bit out of place, a deft and urbane comedienne lost in this moody "film noir" picture, overcast by Aaron Copland's somber score.

# SETTLING DOWN

Myrna Loy heralded the fifties by co-starring with Clifton Webb as the mother of twelve children in *Cheaper by the Dozen* (1950), from the runaway best seller. Frank Gilbreth (Webb) is an efficiency expert and his wife Ernestine (Loy) is the helpmate, a stalwart voice of reason standing between the chaotic demands of her dozen offspring and the childish obstinacy of her husband. He insists on taking pictures during the family's mass tonsillectomy, so Ernestine must help him up the stairs after he passes out from the experience.

Ernestine Gilbreth lectures on psychology and is her husband's business assistant, even taking over after his death. Yet when it comes to family decisions, he is the boss, she merely an assistant coach. Even the children seem to have more power at the family meetings in this zealously pro-life picture. There is a most awkward visit to the Gilbreth home from a representative of family planning, who wants Ernestine to lecture their group. With obvious scorn, Ernestine calls her whole family into the living room to shock the Margaret Sangerite and send her scurrying out the door.

The humor and values of 1950 are somewhat alienating here. Feminists, who find much to cheer about in many Myrna Loy pictures, cannot help but be uncomfortable with *Cheaper by the Dozen*.

Childless again, Loy traveled to England to star in *If This Be Sin* (1950), directed by Gregory Ratoff and scripted by her husband, Gene Markey. As Lady Cathy Brooke, Loy was submerged in a murky melodrama about infidelity and neglect. Cathy has an extramarital affair and later passes the gentleman along to her daughter (Peggy Cummins). Bosley Crowther felt it shameful that so many talented people were sent "knocking about in this film . . . The whole picture ambulates slowly, talks a lot and says nothing at all." Loy's image undergoes a sea change—the perfect wife is transformed into a permanently tarnished angel.

Meanwhile Markey and Loy had separated. She called him "a swell guy," but things just hadn't worked out between them. On June 2, 1951, Loy married Howland Sargeant, an assistant to Dean Acheson in the State Department. (By the early sixties her fourth marriage was kaput. Loy, single today, had permanent marital successes only on the screen.)

In 1952 Loy returned to the screen in *Belles on Their Toes*, a follow-up to *Cheaper by the Dozen*. No longer the passive Ernestine Gilbreth of the first picture, Loy steams at the "absolutely maddening . . . stupid male conceit" which

*CHEAPER BY THE DOZEN (1950). With Clifton Webb*

refuses to "condescend to hire a lady engineer." She is invited to speak at a special dinner at the Engineer's Club in New York. When the chauvinist bridge-builders discover that Dr. Gilbreth is female, however, they send her away. Women aren't allowed in the club. Upset and furious, Ernestine immediately drives her car into a truck and lands in the hospital. Angry Dr. Gilbreth of *Belles on Their Toes* is an enormously appealing character, whom today's feminists could well appreciate. Beyond her busy lecture engagements, teaching assignments, and academic appointment at Purdue the lady finds time to foster her crazy family, still a baker's dozen of kids.

Loy described her next film, *The Ambassador's Daughter* (1956) as "a fun picture to do." As the wife of foolish Senator Cartwright, who wants Paris marked off limits to American soldiers, Loy took second billing to Olivia de Havilland. De Havilland plays the ambassador's misquided daughter, who misguides G.I. John Forsythe into believing she's a French model. Myrna Loy's performance was praised by *New York Times* critic Bosley Crowther, but film historian Leonard Maltin com-

*IF THIS BE SIN (1950). With Richard Greene*

*BELLES ON THEIR TOES (1952). With Jeanne Crain*

mented on the whole that, "Oomph is missing, even though the stars give all to uplift this sagging comedy of de Havilland out for a fling in Paris, romanced by soldier Forsythe."

*The Ambassador's Daughter* was the first time in two decades that Myrna Loy was not given top billing. The message was clear: she would have to get used to smaller parts, joining every other over-forty American actress (but not every actor). She told writer Vernon Scott in 1974, "There's a big ego problem involved in making that transition . . . It was a matter of making up my mind to hang on and wait for star parts—and die of ennui or starvation—or play character roles and keep busy."

Keeping busy has always been important to Loy, who defines her life in terms of work, either on screen or in politics. But working in tinier parts means being extremely selective, choosing roles with integrity. "I won't play those horrible women Bette Davis and Joan Crawford accept," Loy told another writer.

Loy took only unusual roles. In *Lonelyhearts* (1958), derived from Nathanael West's novel *Miss Lonelyhearts*, Loy played the guilt-ridden wife of newspaper editor Robert Ryan. She befriends Montgomery Clift as Adam White,

*THE AMBASSADOR'S DAUGHTER (1956). With Adolphe Menjou and Olivia de Havilland*

author of the paper's advice column, and through him reveals her story of a long-ago infidelity which haunts her still. "*Lonelyhearts*," Loy once reported, "was a film which Monty always thought should never have been released as a commercial movie . . . We all had a great affection for that movie, which Monty thought would have done well concentrated on the art houses."

Apparently Montgomery Clift had some farsighted hope of translating Colette's novel, *Cheri*, into a film, with Loy as the prostitute. But he became ill, and the picture was never made.

Next Loy played Leon Ames's battered alcoholic wife in Mark Robson's CinemaScope adaptation of the John O'Hara novel, *From the Terrace* (1960). She disappeared a quarter of the way through the picture, not long after her son, played by Paul Newman, beat up her lover. The film missed her terribly. She graced it with an energy and intelligence which wooden Joanne Woodward and Newman never mustered. In addition, she seems to be the only character with something besides sex on her mind in this film bursting with late fifties repression. She was off the bottle, but not off drinking in *Midnight Lace* (1960) and *The April Fools* (1969). These roles are informed by Loy's previous cinema characterizations.

In *Midnight Lace*, Loy plays Doris Day's hip Aunt Bea. She jets around the world in search of nothing in particular except a good time and a few old lovers. She arrives in London just when her niece begins to be terrified and tormented by an unseen maniac who turns out to be nasty husband, Rex Harrison. Without Loy around to add some good humor, the pseudo-Hitchcock picture would have been strung out permanently in Day's fever-pitched hysteria.

In *The April Fools* (1969), Loy joins Charles Boyer to form a daffy pair of more-than-middle-aged lovers, married thirty years but behaving as if they'd just found the preacher. Like the old Powell and Loy team, Loy and Boyer are so happy as a couple that they encourage Jack Lemmon and Catherine Deneuve to leave their respective mates and run off together. Loy reads Tarot cards and promises great good fortune to Deneuve, then watches contentedly from a window, with a smile as big as a silver dollar moon, as the April lovers dance in her courtyard below.

In *Airport 1975* (1974), Myrna Loy, nearing her seventieth year, comes aboard as an eccentric lady who survives the mid-air collision by drinking boilermakers and shocking fellow passenger Sid Caesar. Between drinks, she holds

*LONELYHEARTS (1958). With Robert Ryan*

*MIDNIGHT LACE (1960). With Doris Day and John Gavin*

*FROM THE TERRACE (1960). With Paul Newman*

Sid Caesar's hand and comforts him when the in-flight movie, featuring him in a bit part, breaks.

Loy was reunited with Melvyn Douglas for a television version of the creaky 1934 classic, *Death Takes a Holiday*. Loy and Douglas play an aristocratic old couple whose daughter (Yvette Mimieux) flirts with the earthly visitor, Death. Even the enlightened combination of Loy and Douglas couldn't rescue this picture from the grave.

Loy's career never dies. If she is not working in films or fighting for liberal political causes, she is busy in the theater. In 1966 she won the Chicago Sarah Siddons award for playing the addled mother in *Barefoot in the Park*. And in 1972, she appeared on Broadway, again as a mother, in a revival of the thirties play, *The Women*. In 1976, she has made speaking appearances in Washington and New York at retrospectives of her half-century in American movies.

Myrna Loy survives intact and dignified, still beloved and still taken seriously. When once asked her key to this survival, to passing confidently beyond "youthful looks and figure," Loy said that

*THE APRIL FOOLS (1969). With Jack Lemmon*

*AIRPORT 1975 (1974). With Gloria Swanson*

everything depended on remaining optimistic, active and forward-looking. It sounds like a good coda for a phenomenal screen career, which is still happening, lucky for all of us.

Thin chance: but what if William Powell would come out of retirement!

# BIBLIOGRAPHY


Agee, James. *Agee on Film*. New York: Beacon Press, 1964.

Bell, Arthur. "A Drag Queen's Fantasy of a Man's Conception of Women?" *The Village Voice*, June 15, 1972.

Braun, Eric. "Dream Machine, The." *Films and Filming*, March 1974.

———. "Myrna Loy on Comedy." *Films and Filming*, March 1968.

Browning, Norma Lee. "Myrna Loy Waits Eight Years for Right Movie Role." *The Chicago Tribune*, November 17, 1968.

Chierichetti, David. "Myrna Loy Today." *Film Fan Monthly* , 1973.

Everson, William K. *The Detective in Film*. Secaucus, N.J.: Citadel, 1972.

Hammett, Dashiell. *The Thin Man*. New York: Vintage, 1964.

Harrington, Lee. "The Marriage Code of Myrna Loy." *Photoplay*, May 1937.

Hellman, Lillian. "Introduction," *The Big Knockover*, Dashiell Hammett. New York: Vintage, 1972.

Kobal, John. *Gotta Sing Gotta Dance*. New York: Hamlyn, 1970.

Kulik, Karol. *Alexander Korda*. New Rochelle, N.Y.: Arlington House, 1975.

Loy, Myrna. "In This Concluding Chapter of Her Biography Myrna Loy Admits She's Been a Lucky Girl." *The Chicago Daily News*, July 30, 1938.

Marion, Francis. *Off With Their Heads*. New York: Macmillan, 1972.

McBride, Joseph and Wilmington, Michael. "The Wings of Eagles." *The Velvet Light Trap*, No. 2, August 1971.

Mook, S. R. "The Girl Hollywood Can't Beat." *Hollywood*. July 1937.

Parish, James Robert. *Actors Television Credits (1950-1972)*. Metuchen, N.J.: Scarecrow Press, 1973.

———. *Hollywood's Great Love Teams*. New Rochelle, N.Y.: Arlington House, 1974.

Peet, Creighton. Assorted reviews in *The Outlook and Independent*, 1930-1931.

Reed, Rex. "Myrna's Back—and Boyer's Got Her." *The New York Times*, April 13, 1969.

Ringgold, Gene. "Myrna Loy." *Films in Review*, February 1963.

Schickel, Richard. *The Men Who Made the Movies*. New York: Atheneum, 1975.

Sennett, Ted. *Warner Brothers Presents*. New Rochelle, N.Y.: Arlington House, 1971.

Swindell, Larry. *Spencer Tracy*. New York: World, 1969.

Terkel, Studs. *Hard Times*. New York: Avon, 1971.

Thomas, Bob. *Thalberg: Life and Legend*. New York: Doubleday, 1969.

Willis, Donald. *The Films of Frank Capra*. Metuchen, N.J.: Scarecrow Press, 1974.

Wilson, Robert, ed. *The Film Criticism of Otis Ferguson*. Philadelphia: Temple University Press, 1971.

# THE FILMS OF MYRNA LOY

*The director's name follows the release date. A (c) following the release date indicates that the film was in color. Sp indicates Screenplay and b/o indicates based/on.*

*The Silent Years*

1. PRETTY LADIES. MGM, 1925. *Monta Bell.*

2. SATAN IN SABLES. Warner Brothers, 1925. *James Flood.*

3. SPORTING LIFE. Universal, 1925. *Maurice Tourneur.*

4. BEN-HUR. MGM, 1926. *Fred Niblo.*

5. THE CAVEMAN. Warner Brothers, 1926. *Roy Del Ruth.*

6. THE LOVE TOY. Warner Brothers, 1926. *Erle C. Kenton.*

7. THE GILDED HIGHWAY. Warner Brothers, 1926. *J. Stuart Blackton.*

8. WHY GIRLS GO BACK HOME. Warner Brothers, 1926. *James Flood.*

9. THE EXQUISITE SINNER. MGM, 1926. *Josef von Sternberg* and *Phil Rosen.*

10. DON JUAN. Warner Brothers, 1926. *Alan Crosland.*

11. ACROSS THE PACIFIC. Warner Brothers, 1926. *Roy Del Ruth.*

12. THE MILLIONAIRES. Warner Brothers, 1926. *Herman C. Raymaker.*

13. FINGER PRINTS. Warner Brothers, 1927. *Lloyd Bacon.*

14. WHEN A MAN LOVES. Warner Brothers, 1927. *Alan Crosland.*

15. BITTER APPLES. Warner Brothers, 1927. *Harry Hoyt.*

16. THE CLIMBERS. Warner Brothers, 1927. *Paul Stein.*

17. SIMPLE SIS. Warner Brothers, 1927. *Herman C. Raymaker.*

18. HEART OF MARYLAND. Warner Brothers, 1927. *Lloyd Bacon.*

19. A SAILOR'S SWEETHEART. Warner Brothers, 1927. *Lloyd Bacon.*

20. THE JAZZ SINGER. Warner Brothers, 1927. *Alan Crosland.*

21. THE GIRL FROM CHICAGO. Warner Brothers, 1927. *Ray Enright.*

22. IF I WERE SINGLE. Warner Brothers, 1927. *Roy Del Ruth.*

23. HAM AND EGGS AT THE FRONT. Warner Brothers, 1927. *Roy Del Ruth.*

24. BEWARE OF MARRIED MEN. Warner Brothers, 1928. *Archie Mayo.*

25. WHAT PRICE BEAUTY. Pathé, 1928. *Thomas Buckingham.*

26. FANCY BAGGAGE. Warner Brothers, 1929. *John Adolfi.*

27. A GIRL IN EVERY PORT. Fox, 1928. *Howard Hawks.*

28. TURN BACK THE HOURS. Gotham, 1928. *Howard Bretherton.*

29. CRIMSON CITY. Warner Brothers, 1928. *Archie Mayo.*

30. PAY AS YOU ENTER. Warner Brothers, 1928. *John Adolfi.*

31. STATE STREET SADIE. Warner Brothers, 1928. *Archie Mayo.*

32. THE MIDNIGHT TAXI. Warner Brothers, 1928. *John Adolfi.*

33. NOAH'S ARK. Warner Brothers, 1928. *Michael Curtiz.*

*The Sound Years*

34. THE DESERT SONG. Warner Brothers, 1929. *Roy Del Ruth.* Dialogue: Harvey Gates, b/o operetta by Hammerstein and Romberg. Cast: John Boles, Carlotta King, Louise Fazenda.

35. THE BLACK WATCH. Fox, 1929. *John Ford.* Sp. James Kevin McGuiness and John Stone, b/o novel *King of the Khyber Rifles* by Talbot Mundy. Cast: Victor McLaglen, Roy D'Arcy, Cyril Chadwick, Francis Ford.

36. THE SQUALL. Warner Brothers, 1929. *Alexander Korda.* Sp. Bradley King, b/o play by Jean Bart. Cast: Loretta Young, ZaSu Pitts, Alice Joyce, Carroll Nye, Richard Tucker.

37. HARDBOILED ROSE. Warner Brothers, 1929. *F. Harmon Wright.* Sp. Robert Lord, b/o story by Melville Crossman. Cast: William Collier, Jr., Lucy Beaumont, Gladys Blackwell, John Miljan.

38. EVIDENCE. Warner Brothers, 1929. *John Adolfi*. Sp. Edward J. Montagne. Cast: Pauline Frederick, Conway Tearle, Lowell Sherman, Lionel Belmore.

39. SHOW OF SHOWS. Warner Brothers, 1929 (c). *John Adolfi*. Cast: "Floradora Sextette," Alice Day, Lila Lee, Sally O'Neil, Patsy Ruth Miller, Marion Nixon, Lloyd Hamilton, Lupino Lane, Ben Turpin. "Chinese Fantasy," with Nick Lucas.

40. THE GREAT DIVIDE. Warner Brothers, 1930. *Reginald Barker*. Sp: Thomas Dixon, b/o play by William Vaughn Moody. Cast: Dorothy Mackaill, Ian Keith.

41. JAZZ CINDERELLA. Chesterfield, 1930. *Scott Pembroke*. Sp: Arthur Howell and Adrian Johnson, b/o story by Edwin Johns and Oliver Jones. Cast: Frank McGlyn, Nancy Welford, Dorothy Phillips.

42. CAMEO KIRBY. Fox, 1930. *Irving Cummings*. Sp. Marion Orth, b/o play by Booth Tarkington and Harry Leon Wilson. Cast: J. Harold Murray, Norma Terris, Stepin Fetchit.

43. ISLE OF ESCAPE. Warner Brothers, 1930. *Howard Bretherton*. Sp: Lucien Hubbard, b/o story by Jack McLaren. Cast: Monte Blue, Betty Compson, Noah Beery.

44. UNDER A TEXAS MOON. Warner Brothers, 1930. *Michael Curtiz*. Sp: Gordin Rigby, b/o story "Two Gun Man" by Stewart Edward White. Cast: Frank Fay, Raquel Torres, Noah Beery.

45. COCK O' THE WALK. Sono-Art, 1930. *Walter Lang* and *R.W. Neill*. Sp: Nagene Searle and Frances Guihan, b/o novel *Happiness Insurance* by Arturo Mom. Cast: Joseph Schildkraut, Philip Sleeman.

46. BRIDE OF THE REGIMENT. Warner Brothers, 1930. *John Frances Dillon*. Sp: Humphrey Pearson, b/o operetta *The Lady in Ermine*. Cast: Walter Pidgeon, Louise Fazenda, Lupino Lane.

47. LAST OF THE DUANES. Fox, 1930. *Alfred Werker*. Sp: Ernest Pascal, b/o story by Zane Grey. Cast: George O'Brien, Lucile Browne, Nat Pendleton.

48. THE TRUTH ABOUT YOUTH. Warner Brothers, 1930. *William Seiter*. Adaptation: B. Harrison Orkow, b/o H.V. Esmond's *When We Were Twenty-One*. Cast: Loretta Young, David Manners, Conway Tearle.

49. RENEGADES. Fox, 1930. *Victor Fleming*. Sp: Jules Furthman, b/o novel by Andre Armandy. Cast: Warner Baxter, Noah Beery, Bela Lugosi.

50. ROGUE OF THE RIO GRANDE. Sono-Art, 1930. *Spencer Bennet*. Sp:

Oliver Drake. Cast: Jose Bohr, Raymond Hatton.

51. THE DEVIL TO PAY. United Artists, 1930. *George Fitzmaurice*. Sp: Frederick Lonsdale, b/o his play. Cast: Ronald Colman, Loretta Young.

52. THE NAUGHTY FLIRT. Warner Brothers, 1931. *Edward Cline*. Sp: Richard West and Earl Baldwin, b/o story by Frederick Bowen. Cast: Alice White, Paul Page, Robert Agnew.

53. BODY AND SOUL. Fox, 1931. *Alfred Santell*. Sp: Jules Furthman, b/o play *Squadrons* by A. E. Thomas. Cast: Elissa Landi, Charles Farrell, Humphrey Bogart.

54. A CONNECTICUT YANKEE. Fox, 1931. *David Butler*. Sp: William Conselman, b/o novel by Mark Twain. Cast: Will Rogers, William Farnum, Maureen O'Sullivan, Frank Albertson.

55. HUSH MONEY. Fox, 1931. *Sidney Lanfield*. Sp: Dudley Nichols, b/o story by Sidney Lanfield, Courtenay Terrett and Philip Klein. Cast: Joan Bennett, Hardie Albright, Owen Moore.

56. TRANSATLANTIC. Fox, 1931. *William K. Howard*. Sp: Lynn Starling, b/o story by Guy Bolton. Cast: Lois Moran, Greta Nissen, Edmund Lowe, Jean Hersholt.

57. REBOUND. RKO, 1931. *Edward H. Griffith*. Sp: Horace Jackson, b/o play by Donald Ogden Stewart. Cast: Ina Claire, Robert Ames, Hedda Hopper.

58. SKYLINE. Fox, 1931. *Sam Taylor*. Sp: Kenyon Nicholson and Dudley Nichols, b/o novel *East Side, West Side* by Felix Reisenberg. Cast: Thomas Meighan, Maureen O'Sullivan, Hardie Albright.

59. CONSOLATION MARRIAGE. RKO, 1931. *Paul Sloane*. Sp: Humphrey Pearson, b/o story by Bill Cunningham. Cast: Pat O'Brien, Irene Dunne, John Halliday.

60. ARROWSMITH. United Artists, 1931. *John Ford*. Sp: Sidney Howard, b/o novel by Sinclair Lewis. Cast: Ronald Colman, Helen Hayes, Beulah Bondi, A.E. Anson, Richard Bennett.

61. EMMA. MGM, 1932. *Clarence Brown*. Sp: Leonard Praskins, b/o story by Francis Marion. Cast: Marie Dressler, Richard Cromwell, Jean Hersholt.

62. THE WET PARADE. MGM, 1932. *Victor Fleming*. Sp: John L. Mahin, b/o novel by Upton Sinclair. Cast: Dorothy Jordan, Neil Hamilton, Walter Huston, Jimmy Durante, Robert Young.

63. VANITY FAIR. Allied Pictures, 1932. *Chester Franklin*. Sp: F. Hugh Herbert, b/o novel by Thackeray. Cast: Conway Tearle, Barbara Kent, Lionel Belmore.

64. THE WOMAN IN ROOM 13. Fox, 1932. *Henry King*. Sp: Max Marcin and Percival Wilde, b/o play by Samuel Shipman. Cast: Elissa Landi, Ralph Bellamy, Neil Hamilton, Gilbert Roland.

65. NEW MORALS FOR OLD. MGM, 1932. *Charles F. Brabin*. Sp: Zelda Sears and Wanda Tuchock, b/o play *After All* by John van Druten. Cast: Robert Young, Margaret Perry, Jean Hersholt.

66. LOVE ME TONIGHT. Paramount, 1932. *Rouben Mamoulian*. Sp: Samuel Hoffenstein, Waldemar Young, George Marion, Jr., b/o play by Leopold Marchand and Paul Armont. Cast: Jeanette MacDonald, Maurice Chevalier, Charlie Ruggles, Charles Butterworth, C. Aubrey Smith.

67. THIRTEEN WOMEN. RKO, 1932. *George Archainbaud*. Sp: Bartlett Cormack and Samuel Ornitz, b/o novel by A. Tiffany Thayer. Cast: Ricardo Cortez, Irene Dunne, Florence Eldridge, Jill Esmond.

68. THE MASK OF FU MANCHU. MGM, 1932. *Charles F. Brabin*. Sp: Irene Kuhn, Edgar Allan Woolf, and John Willard, b/o novel by Sax Rohmer. Cast: Boris Karloff, Lewis Stone, Karen Morley, Charles Starrett, Jean Hersholt.

69. THE ANIMAL KINGDOM. RKO, 1932. *Edward H. Griffith*. Sp: Horace Jackson, b/o play by Philip Barry. Cast: Ann Harding, Leslie Howard, Ilka Chase, Neil Hamilton.

70. TOPAZE. RKO, 1933. *Harry D'Arrast*. Sp: Benn W. Levy, b/o play by Marcel Pagnol. Cast: John Barrymore, Albert Conti, Reginald Mason.

71. THE BARBARIAN. MGM, 1933. *Sam Wood*. Sp: Anita Loos and Elmer Harris, b/o Edgar Selwyn's *The Arab*. Cast: Ramon Novarro, Reginald Denny, Louise Closser Hale, Edward Arnold.

72. THE PRIZEFIGHTER AND THE LADY. MGM, 1933. *W. S. Van Dyke*. Sp: Frances Marion. Cast: Max Baer, Primo Carnera, Walter Huston, Jack Dempsey.

73. WHEN LADIES MEET. MGM, 1933. *Harry Beaumont*. Sp: John Meehan and Leon Gordon, b/o play by Rachel Crothers. Cast: Ann Harding, Robert Montgomery, Alice Brady, Frank Morgan.

74. PENTHOUSE. MGM, 1933. *W. S. Van Dyke*. Sp: Albert Hackett and Frances Goodrich, b/o story by Arthur Somers Roche. Cast: Warner Baxter, Mae Clarke, Charles Butterworth.

75. NIGHT FLIGHT. MGM, 1933. *Clarence Brown*. Sp: Oliver H. P. Garrett, b/o novel by Antoine de Saint-Exupery. Cast: Helen Hayes, John Barrymore, Clark Gable, Lionel Barrymore, Robert Montgomery.

76. MEN IN WHITE. MGM, 1934. *Richard Boleslavsky*. Sp: Waldemar Young, b/o play by Sidney Kingsley. Cast: Clark Gable, Jean Hersholt, Elizabeth Allan, Otto Kruger.

77. MANHATTAN MELODRAMA. MGM, 1934. *W. S. Van Dyke*. Sp: H. P. Garrett, Oliver T. Marsh, and Joseph L. Mankiewicz, b/o story by Arthur Caesar. Cast: William Powell, Clark Gable, Leo Carrillo, Nat Pendleton, Isabel Jewell.

78. THE THIN MAN. MGM, 1934. *W. S. Van Dyke*. Sp: Albert Hackett and Frances Goodrich, b/o novel by Dashiell Hammett. Cast: William Powell, Maureen O'Sullivan, Nat Pendleton, Minna Gombell, Porter Hall, Cesar Romero, William Henry.

79. STAMBOUL QUEST. MGM, 1934. *Sam Wood*. Sp: Herman J. Mankiewicz, b/o story by Leo Birinski. Cast: George Brent, Lionel Atwill, Mischa Auer.

80. EVELYN PRENTICE. MGM, 1934. *William K. Howard*. Sp: Lenore Coffee, b/o novel by W. E. Woodward. Cast: William Powell, Rosalind Russell, Una Merkel, Harvey Stephens, Isabel Jewell.

81. BROADWAY BILL. Columbia, 1934. *Frank Capra*. Sp: Robert Riskin and Sidney Buchman (uncredited), b/o story by Mark Hellinger. Cast: Warner Baxter, Walter Connolly, Helen Vinson, Douglass Dumbrille, Lynne Overman.

82. WINGS IN THE DARK. Paramount, 1935. *James Flood*. Sp: Jack Kirkland and Frank Partos, b/o story by Neil Shipman and Philip D. Hurn. Cast: Cary Grant, Roscoe Karns, Dean Jagger.

83. WHIPSAW. MGM, 1935. *Sam Wood*. Sp: Howard Emmett Rogers, b/o story by James Edward Grant. Cast: Spencer Tracy, Harvey Stephens, William Harrigan.

84. WIFE VS. SECRETARY. MGM, 1936. *Clarence Brown*. Sp: Norman Krasna, Alice Duer Miller and John Lee Mahin, b/o story by Faith Baldwin. Cast: Clark Gable, Jean Harlow, James Stewart, May Robson.

85. PETTICOAT FEVER. MGM, 1936. *George Fitzmaurice*. Sp: Harold Goldman, b/o play by Mark Reed. Cast: Robert Montgomery, Reginald Owen, Winifred Shotter.

86. THE GREAT ZIEGFELD. MGM, 1936. *Robert Z. Leonard*. Sp: William

Anthony McGuire. Cast: William Powell, Luise Rainer, Frank Morgan, Nat Pendleton, Fannie Brice.

87. TO MARY—WITH LOVE. Twentieth Century-Fox, 1936. *John Cromwell.* Sp: Richard Sherman and Howard Ellis, b/o story by Richard Sherman. Cast: Warner Baxter, Ian Hunter, Claire Trevor.

88. LIBELED LADY. MGM, 1936. *Jack Conway.* Sp: Maurine Watkins, Howard Emmett Rogers and George Oppenheimer, b/o story by Wallace Sullivan. Cast: William Powell, Spencer Tracy, Jean Harlow, Walter Connolly.

89. AFTER THE THIN MAN. MGM, 1936. *W. S. Van Dyke.* Sp: Albert Hackett and Frances Goodrich, b/o story by Dashiell Hammett. Cast: William Powell, James Stewart, Elissa Landi, Sam Levene, Dorothy McNulty (Peggy Singleton).

90. PARNELL. MGM, 1937. *John M. Stahl.* Sp: John Van Druten and S. N. Behrman, b/o play by Elsie T. Schauffler. Cast: Clark Gable, Edna May Oliver, Billie Burke, Donald Crisp.

91. DOUBLE WEDDING. MGM, 1937. *Richard Thorpe.*Sp: Jo Swerling, b/o play *Great Love* by Ferenc Molnar. Cast: William Powell, John Beal, Florence Rice, Jessie Ralph.

92. MAN-PROOF. MGM, 1938. *Richard Thorpe.* Sp: Vincent Lawrence, Waldemar Young and George Oppenheimer, b/o book by Fanny Heaslip Lea. Cast: Franchot Tone, Rosalind Russell, Walter Pidgeon.

93. TEST PILOT. MGM, 1938. *Victor Fleming.* Sp: Vincent Lawrence and Waldemar Young, b/o story by Lieutenant Commander Frank (Spig) Wead. Cast: Clark Gable, Spencer Tracy, Lionel Barrymore, Marjorie Main.

94. TOO HOT TO HANDLE. MGM, 1938. *Jack Conway.* Sp: Laurence Stallings and John Lee Mahin, b/o story by Len Hammond. Cast: Clark Gable, Walter Pidgeon, Walter Connolly, Leo Carrillo, Marjorie Main.

95. LUCKY NIGHT. MGM, 1939. *Norman Taurog.* Sp: Vincent Lawrence and Grover Jones, b/o story by Oliver Claxton. Cast: Robert Taylor, Joseph Allen, Henry O'Neill.

96. THE RAINS CAME. Twentieth Century-Fox, 1939. *Clarence Brown.* Sp: Philip Dunne and Julien Josephson, b/o novel by Louis Bromfield. Cast: Tyrone Power, George Brent, Maria Ouspenskaya, Nigel Bruce, Brenda Joyce.

97. ANOTHER THIN MAN. MGM, 1939. *W. S. Van Dyke.* Sp: Dashiell Hammett. Cast: William Powell, C. Aubrey Smith, Otto Kruger, Nat Pendleton, Virginia Grey.

98. I LOVE YOU AGAIN. MGM, 1940. *W. S. Van Dyke*. Sp: Charles Lederer, George Oppenheimer, and Harry Kurnitz, b/o novel by Leon Gordon and Maurine Watkins. Cast: William Powell, Frank McHugh, Edmund Lowe, Nella Walker.

99. THIRD FINGER, LEFT HAND. MGM, 1940. *Robert Z. Leonard*. Sp: Lionel Houser. Cast: Melvyn Douglas, Raymond Walburn, Lee Bowman.

100. LOVE CRAZY. MGM, 1941. *Jack Conway*. Sp: William Ludwig, Charles Lederer and David Hertz, b/o story by David Hertz and William Ludwig. Cast: William Powell, Jack Carson, Gail Patrick, Florence Bates.

101. SHADOW OF THE THIN MAN. MGM, 1941. *W. S. Van Dyke*. Sp: Irving Brecher, Harry Kurnitz, b/o story by Harry Kurnitz. Cast: William Powell, Donna Reed, Barry Nelson, Sam Levene.

102. THE THIN MAN GOES HOME. MGM, 1944. *Richard Thorpe*. Sp: Robert Riskin and Dwight Taylor, b/o characters created by Dashiell Hammett and story by Robert Riskin and Harry Kurnitz. Cast: William Powell, Lucile Watson, Gloria DeHaven, Anne Revere, Harry Davenport.

103. SO GOES MY LOVE. Universal, 1946. *Frank Ryan*. Sp: Bruce Manning and James Clifden, b/o book *A Genius in the Family* by Hiram Percy Maxim. Cast: Don Ameche, Rhys Williams, Bobby Driscoll.

104. THE BEST YEARS OF OUR LIVES. RKO, 1946. *William Wyler*. Sp: Robert E. Sherwood, b/o novel *Glory for Me* by MacKinlay Kantor. Cast: Fredric March, Dana Andrews, Teresa Wright, Virginia Mayo, Hoagy Carmichael, Harold Russell, Cathy O'Donnell.

105. THE BACHELOR AND THE BOBBY-SOXER. RKO, 1947. *Irving Reis*. Sp: Sidney Sheldon. Cast: Cary Grant, Shirley Temple, Rudy Vallee, Ray Collins.

106. SONG OF THE THIN MAN. MGM, 1947. *Edward Buzzell*. Sp: Steve Fisher and Nat Perrin, b/o characters created by Dashiell Hammett. Cast: William Powell, Keenan Wynn, Dean Stockwell, Phillip Reed, Patricia Morison, Gloria Grahame.

107. THE SENATOR WAS INDISCREET. Universal, 1947. *George S. Kaufman*. Sp: Charles MacArthur, b/o story by Edwin Lanham. Cast: William Powell, Ella Raines, Peter Lind Hayes, Arleen Whelan.

108. MR. BLANDINGS BUILDS HIS DREAM HOUSE. RKO, 1948. *H.C. Potter*. Sp: Norman Panama and Melvin Frank, b/o novel by Eric Hodgins. Cast: Cary Grant, Melvyn Douglas, Sharyn Moffett.

109. THE RED PONY. Republic, 1949 (c). *Lewis Milestone*. Sp: John Steinbeck, b/o his novel. Cast: Robert Mitchum, Louis Calhern, Peter Miles.

110. CHEAPER BY THE DOZEN. Twentieth Century-Fox, 1950 (c). *Walter Lang*. Sp: Lamar Trotti, b/o book by Frank Gilbreth, Jr., and Ernestine Gilbreth Carey. Cast: Clifton Webb, Jeanne Crain, Betty Lynn, Mildred Natwick.

111. IF THIS BE SIN. United Artists, 1950. *Gregory Ratoff*. Sp: Gene Markey, b/o play *Autumn* by Margaret Kennedy and Ilya Surgutchoff Cast: Roger Livesey, Peggy Cummins, Richard Greene.

112. BELLES ON THEIR TOES. Twentieth Century-Fox, 1952 (c). *Henry Levin*. Sp: Phoebe Ephron and Henry Ephron, b/o book by Frank Gilbreth, Jr. and Ernestine Gilbreth Carey. Cast: Jeanne Crain, Jeffrey Hunter, Debra Paget, Hoagy Carmichael, Martin Milner, Edward Arnold.

113. THE AMBASSADOR'S DAUGHTER. United Artists, 1956 (c). *Norman Krasna*. Sp: Norman Krasna. Cast: Olivia de Havilland, John Forsythe, Adolphe Menjou.

114. LONELYHEARTS. United Artists, 1958. *Vincent Donahue*. Sp: Dore Schary, b/o novel by Nathanael West and play by Howard Teichmann. Cast: Montgomery Clift, Robert Ryan, Dolores Hart, Maureen Stapleton.

115. MIDNIGHT LACE. Universal, 1960 (c). *David Miller*. Sp: Ivan Goff and Ben Roberts, b/o play by Janet Green. Cast: Doris Day, Rex Harrison, John Gavin, Roddy McDowall.

116. FROM THE TERRACE. Twentieth Century-Fox, 1960 (c). *Mark Robson*. Sp: Ernest Lehmann, b/o novel by John O'Hara. Cast: Paul Newman, Joanne Woodward, Ina Balin, Leon Ames.

117. THE APRIL FOOLS. National General, 1969 (c). *Stuart Rosenberg*. Sp: Hal Dresner, b/o his story. Cast: Jack Lemmon, Catherine Deneuve, Charles Boyer, Peter Lawford.

118. AIRPORT 1975. Universal, 1974 (c). *Jack Smight*. Cast: Charlton Heston, Gloria Swanson, Karen Black, Sid Caesar, George Kennedy.

*Television Credits:*

1. General Electric Theater, "It Gives Me Great Pleasure." April 3, 1955.
2. General Electric Theater, "The Lady of the House." January 20, 1955.
3. General Electric Theater, "Love Came Late." November 17, 1957.
4. Schlitz Playhouse of the Stars, "No Second Helping." November 22, 1957.

5. "Meet Me in St. Louis." April 26, 1959.

6. June Allyson Show, "Surprise Party." April 18, 1960.

7. Family Affair, February 6, 1967.

8. The Virginian, April 5, 1967.

9. DEATH TAKES A HOLIDAY, October 21, 1971. Film made for television, with Melvyn Douglas.

10. DO NOT FOLD, SPINDLE OR MUTILATE, November 9, 1971. Film made for television.

11. Columbo, "Etude in Black." September 17, 1972.

# INDEX

(Italicized page numbers
indicate photographs)

## ABOUT THE AUTHOR

Karyn Kay attended the University of Wisconsin and Northwestern and teaches film at Livingston College, Rutgers University. She is co-editor of a forthcoming anthology, *Women and the Cinema*, and has contributed to *Film Quarterly*, *Cinema*, *Jump Cut*, and *Film Heritage*, among others. She is a regular writer for *The Velvet Light Trap*.

## ABOUT THE EDITOR

Ted Sennett is the author of *Warner Brothers Presents*, a tribute to the great Warners films of the thirties and forties, and of *Lunatics and Lovers*, on the long-vanished but well-remembered "screwball" movie comedies of the past. He is also the editor of *The Movie Buff's Book*, *The Movie Buff's Book 2*, and *The Old-Time Radio Book*.